Dilemmas
of
Administrative
Behavior

John D. Aram
Cleveland, Ohio

Dilemmas of Administrative Behavior

PRENTICE-HALL, INC., *Englewood Cliffs, New Jersey*

Library of Congress Cataloging in Publication Data

ARAM, JOHN D   1942–
    Dilemmas of administrative behavior.

    Includes bibliographical references.
    1. Decision-making. 2. Management. I. Title.
HD69.D4A72   658.4'03   75–22080
ISBN 0–13–214247–3

© 1976 by PRENTICE-HALL, INC.
Englewood Cliffs, New Jersey

Printed in the United States of America

10   9   8   7   6   5   4   3   2   1

PRENTICE-HALL INTERNATIONAL, INC., *London*
PRENTICE-HALL OF AUSTRALIA, PTY. LTD., *Sydney*
PRENTICE-HALL OF CANADA, LTD., *Toronto*
PRENTICE-HALL OF INDIA PRIVATE LIMITED, *New Delhi*
PRENTICE-HALL OF JAPAN, INC., *Tokyo*
PRENTICE-HALL OF SOUTHEAST ASIA (PTE.) LTD., *Singapore*

Contents

v

5
INDIVIDUAL AND GROUP

6
LEADERSHIP REQUIREMENTS FOR ADHERING TO AND CHANGING GROUP NORMS

7
DIRECTIONS FOR MANAGING DILEMMAS

Preface

Over the course of several years' teaching Organizational Behavior I gradually came to the view that much of the writing in the field emphasizes only one side of an issue. For example, a particular leadership approach might solely promote self-direction, or a particular theory might view organizational members solely in terms of self-interest. While each approach seemed to be valid, each also seemed to be incomplete or to be only partially true. Thus, while organizations require self-direction they also require centralized coordination and direction, and while members do act in terms of immediate self-interest they also assume collective responsibilities. In other words, neither self-direction nor centralized control, self-interest nor collective responsibility is complete in itself. Both sides of these issues are valid in understanding behavior in organizations.

Based on this initial perspective, my ideas developed in several ways. First, it became evident that the administrative literature specifically, and social science thinking in general, supported both sides of many important administrative issues. Thus, the problem of self-interest and collective responsibility had rich antecedents in the thinking of Machiavelli and Rousseau, it was well developed in administrative theory in the works of Cyert and March and Mary Parker Follett, and it was present as an issue in laboratory simulations focusing on competitive/cooperative interpersonal behavior.

Second, it appeared to me that examining issues of organizational behavior in terms of multiple and often conflicting criteria for decision and action was a better approximation of practical realities than theories emphasizing one side of an issue. In developing these chapters I have attempted to stay close to real issues of administration as experienced by managers in all types of organizations. Where possible, I have tried to utilize the experiences of administrators and policymakers by drawing from documents written by or about persons such as Alfred P. Sloan, Senator George Norris, or Admiral Elmo Zumwalt. Occasionally, I have also used a literary figure such as Ibsen's Dr. Stockman to illustrate a point.

The many aspects of administrative theory and the experiences of various managers have been related around the theme of dilemmas. Each of five chapters of this book seeks to explore the tension between two equally important and often mutually exclusive actions. It is hoped these discussions illustrate the multiple criteria present in the behavioral side of administration and some of the complexities of managerial action.

The final development of the book was facing the question of how a manager can deal with a dilemma. What guides can be given for successful coping? Reviewing this question, I found myself in the realm of gestalt psychology and primarily have utilized a gestalt view of individual choice in answering it. In summing up the book I was also drawn to the philosophical implication of a dilemma, namely the presence of existential choice. While not strictly a guide to coping, this discussion seeks to offer a philosophical background to the field of administrative behavior. The psychological and philosophical aspects of administrative dilemmas are discussed in the first and last chapters.

A number of people have given me encouragement, support, and help in the process of writing this book. Suresh Srivastva provided the initial impetus to take on the project as well as personal encouragement along the way. In the early stages of development Jim Waters and Jim Peterson gave enthusiastic reception to my ideas which inspired my confidence and reinforced my efforts. Later, Jim Waters, Peter Reason, and Bob Kaplan all read and commented on the first complete manuscript and I greatly appreciate their painstaking, caring, and helpful suggestions. I also benefited greatly from the comments of John J. Gabarro of Harvard University, Cecil H. Bell, Jr. of the University of Washington, Jerome E. Schnee of Rutgers University, Newark, and Robert E. C. Wegner of the University of Regina. Their suggestions resulted in very significant developments in my thinking and in the coherence of the manuscript. Dave Bachner and Glending Olson gave me helpful writing suggestions, and Sonia Nevis, Gary Robinson, Beth Grady, and Bob Callahan have provided interest and encouragement. Jenny Owens and Lisa Kaplan have shared the typing and numerous retypings of the project and I appreciate their responsive, untiring and quality work. Many other faculty, staff, and students in the Department of Organizational Behavior have been supportive of my efforts. Finally, Dorothy Aram has been an enthusiastic reader of my ideas, an able critic of my writing, and a thoroughly supportive partner in this endeavor. Her interest and support have been essential ingredients in each stage of this project.

Cleveland, Ohio JOHN D. ARAM

Chapter 1

Dilemmas
in Management
conflict and choice

A behavioral scientist, seeking to learn about human behavior, may study a single individual or may focus on a large number of persons. The first approach promises greater knowledge of the complexity of the human being but foregoes the opportunity to generalize across many people. The second approach affords greater generalization but misses the opportunity to know each individual in depth. The development of knowledge requires an understanding of both the particular and the general, although these may call for mutually exclusive approaches to research. How does one best pursue knowledge? No framework for answering this question exists: The researcher is "subjected to pulls in opposite directions" and is required to make a personal choice.[1]

In another area, the leader of a human development group confronts opposing criteria for acting or not acting early in a group's life.[2] On the one hand, a leader who participates actively in a group's early life is likely to increase the dependency of group members—an outcome that is contrary to the goal of personal independence. On the other hand, a leader who is less active and who participates infrequently early in the

---

[1]Abraham Kaplan, *The Conduct of Inquiry: Methodology for Behavioral Science* (San Francisco: Chandler, 1964), p. 30.

[2]Sherman Kingsbury, "Dilemmas for the Trainer," in William C. Dyer, ed., *Modern Theory and Method in Group Training* (New York: Van Nostrand Reinhold, 1972), pp. 107–15.

group may set an example of passivity—also an outcome opposed to the desired norms of a development group. It appears that a leader cannot avoid confronting this situation of equally adverse alternatives.

These situations involve dilemmas for the researcher and the group leader. People in these roles face equally attractive or equally unattractive alternatives, without a way of rationally calculating the "better" choice. Even after a decision in each case has been made and the situation has passed, there is no way for a person to know conclusively if the actual choice was "correct." The ambiguity of a dilemma remains even after an action has been taken.

Actions that are characterized as dilemmas arise on the societal level as well as with individuals. For example, Myrdal's classic, *An American Dilemma*, examined the tension in white America between ideals of equality and freedom and the existing practices of discrimination toward black people.[3] Myrdal perceived a conflict in white America between a desire for social change on the one hand, and on the other hand a desire to maintain social stability. America appeared to want both realization of its ideals *and* preservation of the status quo in racial relationships.

At times, a society may explicitly attempt to change or reform itself. This was the case with social policy in the United States in the early 1960s, as public social agencies were formed to plan for and execute programs intended to alleviate poverty, crime, and inequalities in education and employment in U.S. society.[4] However, planned social reform was found not to be a simple, straightforward matter. Experience of social reform programs showed a conflict between broad-scale community participation and the planning and control of the programs. Several analysts of the private and public thrust for social reform in this period concluded, "The more widely the freedom to initiate change is spread, the more difficult it becomes to control the outcome."[5] Social reformers experienced a dilemma between the value they placed on democratic processes and their desire for concerted action.

Individual and Organization

Modern organizations are typically considered to be plagued with problems, but administrative decisions are not usually thought to consist of opposing criteria that can be considered dilemmas. In the complex

---

[3]Gunnar Myrdal, *An American Dilemma: The Negro Problem and Modern Democracy* (New York: Harper & Row, Harper Torchbooks, 1962).

[4]Peter Marris and Martin Rein, *Dilemmas of Social Reform: Poverty and Community Action in the United States* (New York: Atherton, 1969).

[5]Marris and Rein, *Dilemmas of Social Reform*, p. 235.

relationship of individuals and organizations, there are inherent "pulls in opposing directions" confronting administrators. This individual–organizational relationship is the special domain of the field of administrative behavior, and the dilemmas that arise in organizations are, in part, the content of management.

"The whole is *different* from the sum of the parts"[6] is a major tenet of human perception established by Wolfgang Köhler and other gestalt psychologists. Although this principle was developed in the context of individual perception, paraphrasing it to read, "The organization is different from the sum of its members," conveys a concept important to administration. An organization or collectivity has requirements for its survival and growth that are often distinct from the requirements for its members' security and development. For example, the long-run welfare of the organization may require personal actions that become neglected in favor of more immediate interests of the individual. Likewise, organizational members have needs and interests that do not necessarily coincide with the requirements of maintaining the collectivity. For example, a supervisor's feelings of friendship or animosity toward different subordinates may lead the supervisor to expect different levels of work performance from them.

An administrator or manager typically faces criteria of both individual and organization; as a person, one has personal needs and attitudes that serve to guide action, and as an administrator, one has organizational role obligations that provide guides to ensure the organization's well-being. At times, these criteria are mutually supportive—achievement of one's personal objectives often contributes to organizational objectives and, over time, organizational objectives are necessary for the fulfillment of individual needs. All too often, however, these equally valid and desirable criteria conflict, giving rise to dilemmas of administration. The purpose of this book is to explore these dilemmas and their implications for the practice of management.

Although dilemmas involving individuals and organizations are inherent in administrative decisions, it is important not to oversimplify the individual-versus-organization dichotomy. First, while organizations are legal entities and action is conducted in the name of the whole, organizations are still abstractions—there is no "organizational mind," or something separate from the presence of specific persons. In this sense, it is misleading to conceive of organizations as having needs independent of people. Individuals, however, do hold and act on organizational criteria, and do take actions that coordinate the activities of people associated by

[6]Wolfgang Köhler, *The Task of Gestalt Psychology* (Princeton, N.J.: Princeton University Press, 1969), p. 10.

a formal entity of organization. Even Floyd Allport, a foremost analyst of the relationships of institutions and individuals and a severe critic of the view of institutions as "real," wrote that people do act "as though" institutions are real.[7] Consequently, the dilemma is not a conflict between organizations and individuals; rather, it is a conflict that resides within the thoughts and perceptions of individuals. It is more useful to think in terms of conflicts within people than in terms of a strict dichotomy of individual versus organization.

Furthermore, an organization-versus-individual view is limited and oversimplified because it ignores the interdependent character of individuals and the "organized" contexts in which they work. There is a part/ whole inseparability to the relationship in which each aspect, while different from the other, exists only with respect to the other. Personal independence, for example, is not an individual value that exists in a vacuum: It can be understood only with reference to a social entity external to the person. In this sense, the part is not the whole, but it gains an aspect of its significance in relation to the whole. Similarly, the concept of social organization does not exist irrespective of specific persons. What, if not the benefit of persons, is the ultimate purpose of organizations? Collective values are not ends in themselves, but can be understood only with reference to the experiences and opportunities created for human beings.

The balance that is needed between individual and organizational criteria can be a source of tension within a person or between people. Situations calling for judgments to enhance individual and organization are generally ambiguous. The necessity for immediate action may weaken the perception of interdependence of individuals and organizations and lead to experiencing them in opposition. In addition, the realistic human need to simplify decisions may lead to perceiving one as primary and the other as secondary, heightening the tension rather than the harmony between them. Dealing with the relationship of these criteria, especially in the short run, is the nature of administrative dilemma.

Dilemmas of Administrative Behavior

Chapters 2 through 6 of this book discuss specific administrative dilemmas deriving from this broad relationship of individual and organization. The first three of these five chapters involve the relationship between the in-

---

[7]Floyd Henry Allport, *Institutional Behavior: Essays Toward a Re-Interpreting of Contemporary Social Organization* (Chapel Hill: University of North Carolina Press, 1933), p. 20.

dividual and the organization as a whole. The discussions of these three chapters are based directly on the premise that organizations exist, "as though" they are concrete reality. The remaining two chapters concern the relationship of the individual with face-to-face groups. What follows is a brief summary of each of these five substantive administrative dilemmas.

Self-oriented and collective actions. "What keeps the innumerable conflicting wills [of persons in organizations] from running wild and destroying each other?" asks one social psychologist, grappling with the relation of separate and egocentric individuals to each other.[8] Awareness of the interdependence of persons on each other, or consciousness of a collective responsibility, leads people to moderate and perhaps alter the unfettered exercise of personal will. Yet collective responsibility is rarely an ultimate standard of action, and in practice, immediate self-interests and organizational responsibilities often compete as the basis of one's actions. Specific situations arise in which the private, particular interests of persons and the general interests of organization are both relevant to an individual's actions.

This dilemma of integrating personal and collective interests is a problem of cooperation and trust in interpersonal dealings. For those in positions of broad leadership, this dilemma becomes an issue of the exercise of responsible power: The spoils of private interests become greater and organizational responsibilities become more profound as one's discretion increases.

A dilemma of control and initiative. The structure of tasks and positions in an organization is, in effect, a minimally necessary specification of activities and responsibilities to be performed for organizational survival. Organizations, through the mechanism of hierarchy, and managers, through authoritative actions, attempt to ensure fulfilling these minimal collective needs. But while authority contributes to the performance of tasks and duties, it cannot create, and may in fact inhibit, the initiative and innovation that are also required for long-run survival. The tension between control and initiative is a second specific dilemma inherent to organizational administration.

The issue of authority is usually present on the level of organizational structure as a question of the relative balance of centralization and decentralization. It is also present in the individual/organization relationship in several ways. One of these is the age-old question of leadership: To

[8]Soloman E. Asch, *Social Psychology* (Englewood Cliffs, N.J.: Prentice-Hall, 1952), p. 315.

what extent can supervisory direction and control, which are organizationally necessary, be made consistent with the growth and the innovativeness
of subordinates? Second, the question of authority is present in the in-
dividual/organization relationship in issues concerning the rights of employees and the needs of employers. The rights of individuals to various
freedoms—for example, freedom of privacy—and the needs of employers
to insure a committed and productive work force may at times conflict,
creating another form of administrative dilemma concerning the application of authority.

Personal and institutional criteria.   Just as a manager faces dilemmas
in the application of authority, he or she also confronts administrative
dilemmas in the application of institutional policies and rules and in the
pursuit of the economic goals of an organization.

To the extent that an institution works from a principle of equity,
it seeks to ensure fair dealings between organizational members and to
remove favoritism from administrative decisions. Yet there is an important
role for special needs and considerations of people if organizations are to
maintain any degree of personalness and humanness. Carrying the application of equity too far denies these legitimate claims; placing too great
a value on personal treatment threatens the stability of the institutions.
Administrators who seek to incorporate both these valid criteria face a
difficult dilemma.

In addition to conflicting with standards of equity, human and interpersonal considerations in administrative decisions often conflict with
organizational principles of work efficiency and economy. For example,
the fact that people often help those from whom they have received help
in the past provides a standard for decisions that is quite different from a
strict adherence to the logic of minimal costs. Whereas organizations are
instruments of logic and economy, their members often act in terms of such
reciprocity and in terms of various human and social needs. Possessing
these personal needs and responses, and also holding responsibility for
organizational aims and policies, administrators face an additional set of
dual and often contradictory demands.

Individual needs and group norms.   Groups, universal elements of organization, are commonplace in the experience of organizational members. Group norms are the unwritten and often implicit standards of
behavior or expectations for members, serving to provide continuity and
stability of interaction. Dress codes, norms of punctuality, communication
patterns, and discussion content are only a few examples of the types of
areas in which patterned behavior develops and is maintained in groups.

All groups establish informal structures among members, with those persons most closely adhering to group norms occupying the most central and influential roles. People vary widely in their desire for and acceptance of roles of centrality. To some people, the material, social, or emotional satisfactions of group membership weigh heavily; to others, the autonomy of a more deviant position is highly valued. Although it is not always the case, individuals are frequently faced with a need to balance personal gratifications of being in unity with others against the personal satisfaction of acting autonomously. The former may require a sacrifice of complete independence of action, while the price of the latter may be marginality. Because administrative decisions are often formulated in groups, this personal dilemma has significance in the sphere of management.

Adhering to and changing group norms. As the previous focus was on the individual as group member, the emphasis now changes to the individual as group leader. People in leadership positions require the confidence of group members to maintain their leadership roles, and group members usually express such confidence in terms of adherence to the ideals and norms of the group. At the same time, organizations and groups exist in changing environments, and a second leadership requirement is to ensure the adaptation and survival of the group. At times, adaptation will require modification, alteration, or change in norms of interaction or ways of work in organization. It may also require change in the traditions and values of the members. In these cases, a person faces opposing requirements of leadership—to adhere to and to change group norms. The discussion of specific dilemmas of organizational behavior will conclude with an analysis and discussion of this administrative dilemma.

Method of Studying Dilemmas

Knowledge of these issues is found in academic, professional, and literary fields, so our present method of study will be eclectic. Information will be drawn from writings in the fields of administration, social psychology, social and political theory, philosophy, and fiction. For example, one might find an insight into the nature of a given dilemma in the memoirs of an industrial or government leader, in the conclusions of a poignant laboratory experiment, or in the thoughts of Rousseau, Machiavelli, Bertrand Russell, or Herman Melville. Each chapter is an attempt to draw together diverse materials to focus and define the central dilemma and to show its presence in a variety of contexts. If preferences for particular types of sources exist, they are for laboratory studies in social psychology and for the actual experiences of organizational leaders. Throughout, an emphasis is placed on the choices faced by individuals; the individual in the large organization is the central perspective guiding this study.

An Approach to Viewing Organizational Behavior

Historically, behavioral scientists' studies of administration have been based on the assumption that a particular behavior leads to a particular outcome, an approach that has generally led to inconclusive results. For example, the question of whether participative leadership improves worker performance has been the focus of a great deal of research.

Recently, a movement toward studying contingencies of behavior has gained strong emphasis. If one learns the importance and nature of such conditions as worker needs, organization structure, task requirements, and so forth, the relationship of variables such as leadership and performance will be clarified. Effective administrative behavior, in this view, is contingent on a given set of specific circumstances.

The contingency approach and the perspective of dilemmas in organizational behavior share a repulsion to simple principles of human administration: In each approach, the specific situation is paramount and universal solutions are avoided. They differ, however, in that the contingency approach assumes that conditions of leadership or organization structure can ultimately be specified exactly and thoroughly. It also assumes that a particular solution is optimal for a particular situation—that the problem of administrative behavior is solely one of gaining sufficient knowledge.

The present approach agrees with those who acknowledge the absence of optimal solutions and who see the existence of trade-offs among alternatives. This viewpoint assumes the presence of equally valid and yet conflicting forces. Its presumption is that the tension of individual and organizational requirements will never be resolved finally or optimally; choice as well as knowledge is the nature of administrative behavior.

Relevance of Administrative Dilemmas to Management

The solution of dilemmas. Can a dilemma ever be resolved? Dilemmas pose a different challenge from those of most organizational problems. One definition of a problem is a discrepancy between an ideal and an actual state. Much of management problem solving consists of conducting rational analyses to reduce this discrepancy. But since dilemmas do not yield to rational operations in this way, they are not solvable in the same sense that many other organization problems are.

A dilemma may be closer to a paradox. A paradox is a statement or situation containing a logical contradiction. For example, the mathematical proof known as Arrow's Paradox shows that under certain conditions, a purely egalitarian society cannot arrive at a majority decision. The contradiction is that, therefore, in at least one logical situation, a self-governing society cannot govern.

Although a paradox conveys a logically contradictory state of affairs, it offers no choice to be made, no action to be taken. A dilemma, on the other hand, is an opposition in which choice is necessary. A dilemma is a predicament—a complicated and perplexing situation—that requires choice between equally valued alternatives.

The fact that only reasonable trade-offs are possible in coping with dilemmas does not lessen the importance of the ideal of both individual and organizational fulfillment. This ideal, which is unattainable according to the strict business of practical affairs, allows people to tie specific actions to a higher purpose. The presence of an ideal of human invention and striving provides an end point by which to convey meaning to action. Ideals, as fictions or imaginary conceptions, have been argued to be vital to life. This philosophical view is stated by German philosopher Hans Vaihinger:

> Without [fictional ideals] the satisfaction of understanding, the ordering of our chaotic material, would be impossible; without them all advanced science would be impossible, for they serve as its instruments both in the process of thought and in the preparatory stages; without them, finally, all higher morality would be impossible.[9]

In other words, the unattainable ideal is a positive, vital force in life that provides a point outside direct human experience to create meaning, advance knowledge, and judge acts. It is in this spirit that the unsolvable nature of a dilemma has a key significance.

Guides to coping with dilemmas. Given the unsolvable nature of dilemmas, what guidelines can be given managers for coping? What personal qualities are relevant to this management task? While guidelines are

[9]Hans Vaihinger, *The Philosophy of 'As If': A System of the Theoretical, Practical and Religious Fictions of Mankind* (New York: Harcourt Brace Jovanovich, 1924), p. 50.

anything but plentiful, there are several ways to enhance one's ability to cope with dilemmas.

An initial guide lies in the mental orientation of an individual toward action. One orientation is to experience the poles of a dilemma as choices extending outward from a situation. The person in this situation views the possibility of action in either direction and holds open the potential for action on either criterion. This position is an involved but initially uncommitted posture: it is maintaining an "interested impartiality." Action is uninfluenced by one's previous actions and is related totally to the immediate situation.

However, rarely are we free of partiality in facing the issues posed by these dilemmas. Most of us tend, *a priori*, to be committed to either an individualist or a collectivist creed, inclined toward personal or institutional criteria, toward change- or tradition-oriented roles in groups, and so forth. As a product of either growing-up experiences or habitual ways of acting, people often have patterned ways of responding to dilemma situations. To be impartial often means to withdraw one's involvement.

Where one has "standing" commitments to particular criteria, the process of choice is often tiring and full of tension. People in this case essentially feel themselves to be at the center of counteracting forces—while the preferred criterion exerts a strong force in one direction, the opposing criterion resists or counteracts this action. To act on one's preferred criterion means to overcome the forces in the other direction. This orientation consumes considerable mental and emotional energy in the struggle of forces. An orientation of "interested impartiality," on the other hand, does not require energy to maintain supremacy of one's preferred criterion. Breaking of habitual responses makes either alternative emotionally plausible and ties up one's energy less in a conflict of forces. One acts—and then is free to act in a similar or different way in a succeeding dilemma of the same type. Consequently, the guide for a practicing manager is not how to act in a dilemma situation, but rather how to orient oneself to the problem of choosing.

A second way of approaching dilemmas is to apply Barnard's "invention of concrete solution." In this process, the complicated and perplexing nature of a dilemma leads one to create an alternative to existing choices. For example, if the use of a particular medical drug has strong deleterious side effects, a physician faces a dilemma in its use: whether to create as serious a medical situation as the initial problem, or to leave the patient's condition untreated. In many cases, this conflict has led the medical profession to discover new drugs that have the same therapeutic effect without the same side effects. Although an immediate decision is still imperative in a dilemma situation, it may often be possible to take future actions that prevent a specific dilemma from recurring.

The Philosophical Implication of Administrative Dilemmas

There is today no universal theory of administration. There is rather a great diversity of viewpoints, concepts, tools of analysis, and prescriptions for managers. This book seeks to illuminate a particular viewpoint about organizations, which implies that one of the tasks of management is existential choice. One leading writer about general management has stated, "Every act, every decision, every deliberation of management, has economic performance as its first dimension,"[10] but the viewpoint here is that dilemmas of administrative behavior are not reducible to economic or any other *a priori* method of analysis. Rather, they stand in their own right as independent and distinct personal choices.

"Man is condemned to be free," wrote Jean-Paul Sartre. By this he meant that life has nothing within it or outside it that *a priori* establishes good, truth, or meaning: "There is no explaining things away by reference to a fixed and given human nature . . . [Man] is responsible for every thing he does."[11] The point is relevant to administrative dilemmas: One's choices are uniquely personal, not justifiable in terms of the logic of economics or the obligations of official protocol. Existential choice is inherent in organizations and is one of the tasks of management.

Sartre presents an example of a young Frenchman facing an existential choice with opposing pulls resembling those of the dilemmas discussed here. The young man was a student during the Second World War. His older brother had been killed earlier in the war, and the student desired revenge for his death. He lived alone with his mother; his father was a collaborator with the German forces. Sartre states:

The boy was faced with the choice of leaving for England and joining the Free French Forces—that is, leaving his mother behind—or remaining with his mother and helping her to carry on. He was fully aware that the woman lived only for him and that his going off—and perhaps his death—would plunge her into despair. He was also aware that every act that he did for his mother's sake was a sure thing, in the sense that it was helping her to carry on, whereas every effort he made toward going off and fighting was an uncertain move which might run aground and prove completely useless; for example, on his way to England he might, while passing through Spain, be detained indefinitely in a Spanish camp; he might reach England

---

[10]Peter F. Drucker, *Management: Tasks, Responsibilities, Practices* (New York: Harper & Row, 1974), pp. 40–41.

[11]Jean-Paul Sartre, *Existentialism and Human Emotions* (New York: Philosophical Library, 1957), pp. 22–23.

or Algiers and be stuck in an office at a desk job. As a result, he was faced with two very different kinds of action: one, concrete, immediate, but concerning only one individual; the other concerned an incomparably vaster group, a national collectivity, but for that very reason was dubious, and might be interrupted en route.[12]

Sartre argues that there is no conclusive religious or ethical guide to the young man's choice; Sartre's own response to him is, "You're free, choose; that is, invent."

Existentialists have not looked kindly on organizations as the source of choice and human invention. Typically in existentialist novels, organizations are mammoth bureaucracies representing impersonal and antihuman forces.[13] The existential focus is on the one who is against these forces. The present study focuses on people working within institutions. This is a matter of personalizing the object of existentialist novels, the bureaucrat, and reapplying the context for existential choice. The dilemmas discussed here are not resolved by recourse to external reference points but demand personal, existential decision.

Choosing within a dilemma is not simply an administrative task. On the contrary, choice is a statement in favor of the human potential for creativity. The presence of choice in the nature of dilemmas places administration in the realm of what is uniquely human—to create meaning through the exercise of autonomy. In this manner, at least, administration carries philosophical relevance. A final perspective on dilemmas of administrative behavior is to draw forth this significance.

CHAPTER REVIEW

This chapter has sought to introduce the reader to the concept of dilemmas in the area of administrative behavior. It has been argued that opposing criteria for administrative action are inherent in the very nature of social organizations, and that these criteria comprise existential dilemmas. The organization and the methodology of the following five chapters have been outlined briefly; the role of dilemmas in the study of administrative behavior and their relevance to management have been discussed. Finally, we have taken a brief look at guidelines for coping with dilemmas and at their philosophical relevance, issues to which we will return in Chapter 7.

---

[12]Sartre, *Existentialism*, pp. 24–25.
[13]For example, the calculating and impersonal supervisor in Camus's *The Stranger*, or the impenetrable layers of rules, structures, and directives of Kafka's *The Castle*.

Chapter 2

Individual
and Collective Interests
the dilemma of meeting self-interest
versus
fulfilling collective responsibility

In his analysis of the relation of individuals and societies, Jean-Jacques Rousseau argued that the central issue was "To find a form of association which may defend and protect ... the person and property of every associate, and by means of which each ... may nevertheless obey only himself, and remain as free as before."[1] Transposed into terms of modern organizational problems, this statement might read, "... to develop organizations that fulfill the needs of individuals without requiring them to forego personal preference." Rousseau had a unique response to the issue: He postulated the existence of a "general will" that allows both a strong collectivity and individual freedom. The general will is "each person giving himself to all"[2]—that is, each person acting completely in the public interest. Rousseau believed that if people were given adequate information, the "best" judgments of all individuals, privately expressed, would be close in outcome and would comprise the general will or the common interest. He thought that collectivities of people err in allowing private interests, factions, and special interests to cause deviations from the general will.

Private interests, factions, and special interests are common aspects of organizational behavior and frequently provide criteria for decisions.

[1]Jean-Jacques Rousseau, *The Social Contract* (New York: Simon & Schuster, 1967), pp. 17–18.
[2]Rousseau, *The Social Contract*, p. 18.

13

In terms of practical influence, Rousseau's "general will" is a long way from being a concrete and dominant concept of administration. Yet the concept is not entirely hypothetical. Most people do feel collective responsibilities and do act on the basis of a perceived organizational or "public" interest. In organizations, individual interests such as financial gain or personal power are normal and expected; extending them beyond "reasonable" levels, however, leads to the detriment of the whole organization. Many decisions rely on the individual's ability to balance private interests with self-restraint.

The degree of emphasis one places on self-restraint or on self-gratification gives rise to different philosophies of life. Spiritual societies are probably good examples of associations based on ideals of collective responsibility and selflessness. On the other hand, the philosophies of hedonism and epicureanism stress sensual gratification and seek to maximize individual pleasure. Emphasis on collective welfare and emphasis on individual welfare have distinct appeals, and each has attracted its adherents. While some people seek a way of life at one extreme or the other, most people's actions place individual interests paramount at some times and make group or organizational interests primary at others. Only rarely does a person act wholly one way or wholly the other.

These philosophical positions are present in choices people face in organizations. A person may lean toward acting in the interests of a group or toward taking advantage of opportunities for personal gain. The former tendency may require relatively more personal sacrifice; the latter may forfeit collective needs. Collective responsibility and private interests are inevitable criteria for action in organizations; sometimes they coincide, and sometimes they conflict. Organizations seek ways of alleviating the potential tension between them. For example, many compensation systems, such as retirement plans, are designed to bring together the individual's financial interests and the organization's need for a stable manpower force. Also, most organizations understand the limits to which self-oriented behavior may prevail. Such "rules of the game" might relate to the extent that expense accounts can be padded, or the extent that purchasing agents are influenced by personal contributions of vendors.

The definition of "interests" can be highly ambiguous: Is it in a person's interest to undertake additional work that promises no personal gain but contributes to the group effort? Is a department's interest best met by working on broad organizational problems, or on narrower departmental problems where costs are more controllable, success more easily achieved, and recognition more readily gained? Does an organization's interest lie with additional expenditures in socially oriented projects, or additional expenditures in equipment modernization? From the acts of individuals to the policies of nations, the definition of "interests" is a difficult and consequential problem.

To a large extent, the dilemma is an issue of one's time perspective. A person may act to gain immediate benefits or to gain future benefits. Collective interests lead one to assume responsibilities, do work, or forego gratifications now in order to preserve, maintain, or strengthen the group or organization from which future benefits are expected. If an organization is to be an enduring association, its long-term interests need to be observed to some extent in the day-to-day actions of its members. Of course, as a person's role carries more general responsibility, longer-range concerns will naturally receive greater emphasis. Also, to the extent that a person expects to have a continuing relationship with an organization, he or she will be more open to broad interests.

Self-interest and collective responsibility are alternative and often contradictory criteria for individual actions in organizations. The point of entry into this problem is a discussion and contrast of two well-developed theories of organization: One view emphasizes the self-interest side of human nature, describing organizational behavior in terms of coalitions and processes of bargaining; the other view stresses integrative behavior and the need for members to assume organizational responsibility. The following section discusses these two positions; it attempts to show that each contains an aspect of organizational reality and that multiple and competing levels of interests exist in organizations.

The discussion then turns to the problem of establishing cooperation within any one level of organization—say, individuals within a group or a department. Establishment of cooperation is seen as a problem of trust in the other's intentions and implies vulnerability or risk. The dilemma of trust, studied in small group experiments, is seen to have a counterpart in the experience of organizational members.

A final section of this chapter deals with the dilemma of power and responsibility. We will examine the dual needs in leadership, for discretion in order to fulfill general responsibilities, and for close accountability in order to constrain potential abuses of power. Related to this issue will be a discussion of the tension in political affairs between public and constituent interests. Here special reference will be given to Senator George Norris's pursuit of public power in the 1920s in the United States. Finally, the problem of ends and means is examined through the writings of Niccolò Machiavelli. A review of *The Prince* not only shows Machiavelli's candid pragmatism of administrative self-interest; it also reveals his own ideals of Italian unification and nationalism. From *The Discourses* is gained additional support for Machiavelli's emphasis on the leader's responsibility for the cohesiveness and unity of state, and the desirability for the leader to act in a selfless manner. Rather than resolving the self/ collectivity dilemma, Machiavelli is seen to provide a historical, but also highly relevant, example of tension between the instincts of the ambitious person who can and does achieve power and the society's or organization's need for selfless acts of leadership.

Two Views of Organizations

Theorists have held very diverse views about the bases of members' actions in organizations. This section reviews two prominent and quite different theories. One, based on a self-interest assumption about individuals, sees organizations as coalitions, and administrative leadership as, at least partially, a process of coalition management. Another view is established on the premise that taking collective responsibility is both possible and desirable. The function of organizational leadership in this perspective is to unite all participants in a common purpose and to encourage their identification and unification with the whole enterprise. On the one hand, organizations are seen as quasi-stable coalitions, and on the other hand, as integrative unities. Close examination will show that the views together are a better conceptualization of organizational behavior than either alone, and that choice is inherent in the tension between collective and self-responsibility.

   Organizations and coalition bargaining. An organization can be defined as a set of individually held contracts: The relation of an individual to an organization is the performance of specified work in return for money, status, security, authority, and so forth. But organizations are also goal-directed systems. The question then arises, How can we understand the emergence of general goals from a set of individually held contracts?

   The solution to this problem is found in the idea of coalitions. Individuals, once employed, have different interests, or preference orderings, that lead them to prefer certain organizational goals over other organizational goals. Like-minded people join together in coalitions and enter bargaining processes with other coalitions relevant to goal setting.[3] Bargaining is the process of resolving inherent conflict, at least to a satisfactory degree. The stakes of the bargaining process are not only monetary and prestige interests, but also policy and goal commitments. Thus, goals and policy are outcomes determined by interaction. The necessary conditions for organizational functioning are (1) individuals' decisions to

[3]Richard M. Cyert and James G. March, *A Behavioral Theory of the Firm* (Englewood Cliffs, N. J.: Prentice-Hall, 1963).

participate, indicated through employment contracts, (2) the identification of individual interests that allow for the formation of coalitions, and (3) the willingness of coalitions to engage in the give-and-take of bargaining.[4] There is an assumption of inevitable conflict that is resolved, at least in part, through domination of the stronger coalition and through compromise between equally strong coalitions.

This discussion is drawn primarily from *A Behavioral Theory of the Firm*, by Richard Cyert and James March. In addition to this basic conception, these authors see goals and commitments achieving a semipermanent status in organizations that provides for stability and continuity. Day-to-day bargaining goes on but is largely an elaboration and clarification of objectives within constraints provided by precedent. Cyert and March state, "Much of the structure is taken as given. This is true primarily because organizations have memories in the form of precedents, and individuals in the coalition are strongly motivated to accept the precedents as binding."[5] This condition avoids continuous negotiation on all organizational commitments. In this sense, past bargains, for better or worse, influence present bargaining, and "The 'accidents' of organizational genealogy tend to be perpetuated."[6]

The coalition theory of organizations has been extended by James D. Thompson, writing in the Cyert and March tradition.[7] Thompson states that the conventional image of an all-powerful individual at the top of an organization, setting goals and controlling activities, is at best only true for simple situations in which technology is standardized and predictable. Similarly, such omnipotence is possible only where the various technological, social, and economic environments of the organization are stable. Where internal technologies are uncertain and environmental factors changing—namely, in *complex* management situations—the assumption of an omnipotent individual gives way to the presence of organizational coalitions. In fact, the more sources of uncertainty and contingency within the organization and outside it, the more internal power bases there are and the greater political activity becomes. The more complex the management task, the more obvious will be coalitions in the organization.

Stability is provided to the organization as a whole, in Thompson's view, not so much by organizational precedent as by the emergence of a dominant coalition. For example, in some businesses, people holding a marketing viewpoint may be dominant, and their continuity gives the

---

[4]Cyert and March, *A Behavioral Theory*, pp. 26–43.
[5]Cyert and March, *A Behavioral Theory*, p. 33.
[6]Cyert and March, *A Behavioral Theory*, p. 34.
[7]James D. Thompson, *Organizations in Action* (New York: McGraw-Hill, 1967).

organization stability. Yet, several additional organizational processes are necessary to mitigate potential conflict, direct energy, and coordinate activities in complex organizations. One of these is an *inner circle*, either formal or informal, to work out necessary compromises between coalitions. Second, Thompson argues that a *central power figure* will emerge in situations of widely distributed power. Not having unilateral power, this person will nevertheless exercise significant leadership in the adjudication and coordination of coalition interests. This person, in Thompson's words, is the "superb politician." He states, "Without the 'superb politician,' metropolitan school systems, urban governments, universities, mental hospitals, social work systems, and similar complex organizations would be immobilized."[8] As with the view of conflict resolution of Cyert and March, Thompson views compromise, and to some extent domination, as the primary means of conflict resolution in organizations. None of these writers treats as significant a concept of collective responsibility or action based on the perception of the organization's need as a whole.

Organizations and integrative unity.   A counterpoint to this view of organizations is the "integrative unity" perspective of Mary Parker Follett.[9] Applying her analysis to the issues of public and private enterprises of her day, Mary Follett developed an alternative view of the manner in which individual and group interests can be formulated in organizations and of the process of conflict resolution.

Follett illustrates how self-interest might take on different meanings, depending on the perspective the persons assume, or the level of organization with which they identify. For example, persons accept jobs that meet immediate economic and personal interests. Now they join a union and identify their interests with the fate of others through collective action. In this case, self-interest takes on a broader meaning, as the persons may forego some personal flexibility in the interest of the union's strength. Another step might be taken if the union and management join forces to solve industrial relations problems. Again, the meaning of self-interest has been redefined by the employees, as it now becomes intertwined with the organization's needs as well as the union's interests. Follett's plea is for seeing the self as a conscious element of the whole. She states:

> . . . What I am urging is that we should be as interested, as self-interested, as possible, but only as members of the highest unity with which we are capable of identifying ourselves.[10]

---

[8]Thompson, *Organizations in Action*, p. 143.
[9]Mary Parker Follett, *Dynamic Administration: The Collected Papers of Mary Parker Follett*, eds. Henry C. Metcalf and L. Urwick (New York: Harper & Row, 1940).
[10]Follett, *Dynamic Administration*, p. 218.

The case for merging individual and organizational interest is partly based on the perspective of "the long run." To the extent that an individual is related to an organization over time, in the long run the organization's interest is the individual's interest.

Yet the attitude is not only a temporal definition of one's interest. There can be and is often simply an identification with the good of the whole or the community. Follett makes this point through a personal example:

> Once I was being rowed, with a friend, across Lake Como on a summer day at noon. We were all good-sized people, it was an exceptionally hot day, and the rower became about the hottest looking man I ever saw. I summoned up enough Italian to try to express my sympathy for him, to deplore the heat. He looked at me in amazement and replied, "But it's good for the vines." Probably he had no vines himself, but he had identified himself with the community interest. It was not that he was willing to suffer for the good of all, he saw his own interest included in that of all, even although he probably could not have put it into words.[11]

Idealistic as a general premise of organizational behavior? Yes. Yet the degree to which consciousness of unity is fostered throughout an organization may be a factor in its effectiveness.

The management task in integrative theory is not adjudication and coordination between conflicting coalitions. Rather, it is a process of mutual interaction among parties and of attempts to integrate or unify the various contributions of people and groups. Collective responsibility, in Follett's view, is a feeling of "being responsible for a functional whole," as opposed to "being responsible for a function in a whole." Collective responsibility is illustrated by one department's meeting to discuss how it can better help other departments execute their functions, or by the attitude that a person can be "*for* labor without being *against* capital; you can be for the institution."[12]

Follett's view contains an implicit statement of effective conflict resolution. Conflict and conflict resolution are processes of great significance to integrative unity, and Follett consequently devotes close attention to them. In her view, conflict is an inevitable and necessary aspect of human affairs; in fact, she states that conflicts are the "essence of life." At the same time, it is possible for conflict to be constructive, creative, and integrative.

An example of this integrative conflict resolution is provided by a

[11]Follett, *Dynamic Administration*, p. 217.
[12]Follett, *Dynamic Administration*, p. 82.

rather simple but clear example of the problem of how dairymen were to unload their milk cans at the creamery platform of the Dairyman's Cooperative League.[13] It seems that the creamery was on a hill and was serviced by dairymen coming from either up or down the hill. Both the "uphillers" and the "downhillers" claimed priority in unloading cans at the creamery platform, creating a controversy that raged to the point of disruption. The advice of an outsider provided the solution of changing the position of the platform so that both groups could unload simultaneously. A constructive and integrative solution was possible, although not immediately obvious to the parties, in a situation that might typically have had to be resolved by power domination or by compromise.

    Coalition and integration compared.   The concept of integrative unity is aspirational. Mary Parker Follett appears to project one aspect of behavior into a dominant role in organizations. Her writing seems to urge or encourage organizational members to achieve that which *might be*. Writers in the coalition-theory tradition, on the other hand, appear to describe what *is*, and seem relatively unconcerned about what could be different or "better." The desire to describe and to predict leads to the realities of political behavior as a central focus.

    And yet, can it not also be said that organizations frequently suffer from the pursuit of narrow individual and group interests, and that coalitions, whether departmental, management/labor, professional, or whatever, often seem to interfere with the effective operation of the whole enterprise? In other words, while self-interested behavior and coalition interests are typical of people's experience in organizations, they can and often do appear to impede overall organizational effectiveness.

    Of course, these two approaches are not mutually exclusive; both are bases for people's actions in organizations. Groups, departments, and even whole organizations develop solidarity and cohesiveness. There are loyalties and identifications at each level of membership. Observations from experimental studies suggest that interpersonal cooperation begins when people perceive their goals to be interdependent. The experience of cooperation, initiated on a self-interest basis, increases the interest of each person in the other's welfare and may lead to affective bonds between people. Consequently, loyalty and solidarity can be generated out of self-interest intentions and can become independent of an initial relationship. Viewing organizations solely in terms of exchange, personal interests, and opportunistic behavior does not account for the development of such loyalties and feelings of group identification.

    However, group loyalties may not be completely integrative either.

---

[13]Follett, *Dynamic Administration*, pp. 32–33.

To a degree, group identifications become group interests and may be obstacles to members' identification with departmental and total organizational interests. In this sense, group loyalty at one level of organization can itself become a private interest from the perspective of more encompassing organizational units. Needs and interests at different vertical levels of an organization may conflict and thus be incapable of being simultaneously met. That integration at one level can often be experienced as a self-interested coalition from another level requires an acceptance of both processes in understanding administrative behavior.

The Trust Dilemma

The problem of trust in organizational behavior. Competing interests in organizations are practically universal. Departmental interests differ within universities, hospitals, business, and governments, and a central question becomes, What set of priorities between departments represents the well-being of the organization? The same problem exists for individuals in relation to group objectives. Each person has different task preferences, special abilities, and personal preferences; what work assignments reflect the best combination of efforts? A certain degree of departmental or group-member competitiveness may be motivating and may aid the achievement of broader goals. However, beyond some point, competition often becomes debilitating to constructive work.

Cooperative behavior recognizes situations as composed of oneself *and* others, and acts of cooperation attempt to assure the well-being of all parties. Cooperative behavior also assumes that the other will see the situation in the same way. There is risk in any cooperative action, since the other person may not hold similar assumptions and may not reciprocate. In this case, a person's position may be worse than if a competitive stance had been taken. For example, a department head who provides departmental cost figures to other department heads in the expectation of cooperation may find not only a lack of reciprocation, but also the use of such information in arguments that his own departmental budget should be reduced. Or a group member who brings conflict into the open may discover that others are unwilling to participate and may find a lack of cooperation in resolving group problems. A cooperative attitude implies risk or vulnerability to the intentions of others; cooperation is, by definition, a collective process. It is a delicate attitude that is often developed and maintained only through deliberate and continuous effort.

The assumption that others will reciprocate an act of cooperation implies trust. Trust is a necessary element to weld intergroup and interindividual interests into a united, smoothly functioning whole. It is the essential ingredient of integrative unity, and a very elusive quality in organizational behavior.

The dilemma of trust is clearly depicted in what has become known as the Prisoner's Dilemma game. This game is derived from the general theory of games developed by Luce and Raiffa.[14] The game gets its name from the situation in which two persons are held for allegedly committing a crime. They are interrogated separately, and each is promised a light sentence for turning state's witness. If neither person acquiesces, only insufficient evidence exists, and both are released on minor charges. If both defect, each receives a moderate sentence. If one defects and the other trusts, the trusting person "gets the book thrown at him."

In its simplest form, this game is played by two people who each face two choices, as shown below:

		Person B	
		Strategy I	Strategy II
Person A	Strategy I	$(+5, +5)$	$(-4, +6)$
	Strategy II	$(+6, -4)$	$(-3, -3)$

In this game, both players can secure five points by taking Strategy I, but to do so requires mutual trust. If one party "trusts" and the other "defects," the trusting person receives a heavy penalty of minus four points. If both attempt to defect, they both receive a penalty.

While the dilemma of trust may not apply widely to prisoners, this problem describes common situations in administration. Frequently, a person wonders to what extent another can be counted upon to put out the extra effort to complete a task, or to give agreement in public to ideas that were privately supported, or to communicate work problems in an equally open manner. To what extent, one might ask, is cooperation limited by my own orientation toward trust? If I act cooperatively, will others follow, or do I stand to be exploited? The experience of having someone else "defect" when one "trusts" is particularly frustrating and anger-provoking, while the experience of having another also "trust" generally builds liking and positive feeling.

Joint tasks and interdependent work occur constantly in organizations, and they demand some type of relationship between people. Relationships can be more or less cooperative, individualistic, or competitive, depending on the orientations of the people involved. The benefits of cooperation, usually greater relationship satisfaction and

---

[14]R. Duncan Luce and Howard Raiffa, *Games and Decisions* (New York: John Wiley, 1957).

greater work progress, can be attained only as people are able to affirm each other's willingness to trust. But the affirmation of trust is not automatic; defecting may have its benefits too, and is enough of a possibility so that trust always implies risk. The dual desire to have a cooperative relationship and to protect oneself from vulnerability creates a dilemma of choice.

Several inferences from laboratory studies. Experimental research using the Prisoner's Dilemma game has been voluminous. Behavior of subjects has been studied with different payoff matrices, different numbers of people, different patterns of communication, different patterns of announcing decisions, and so forth. Two of the findings from this series of studies appear particularly relevant to organizational behavior. First, several studies have shown strong noncooperative patterns in their results. With no particular orientation to the relationship, pairs of people in the Prisoner's Dilemma have been found to take "cooperative" strategies a low percentage of the time. One reviewer of this effect commented, "The utility of beating an opponent has a higher value in these games than winning money."[15] This noncollaborative effect appears to persist even when subjects have a consistently trusting partner. One study arranged for a player to take Strategy I over nearly all of the trials of the game. Concern for the other's welfare appeared low, as suggested by one observer of this study: "... even a 95 percent cooperative opponent fails to induce over 50 percent cooperative play on the part of the subject."[16] Apparently, the 5 percent of the time in which the confederate was not "trusting" was sufficient reason for the subjects to avoid vulnerability of their own positions. These experimental results are far removed from organizations, but if they have any approximation to experience outside the laboratory, they suggest a bias toward the protective rather than the risky side of the dilemma of trust.

A second experimental finding of interest was from a study that introduced a third party. Both players of the Prisoners' Dilemma were real subjects; the third person was an experimental accomplice who, in an exercise prior to the game, acted in a conspicuously "obnoxious and irritating" manner in the presence of the subjects.[17] The purpose was to create a dislike for this third person by two subjects and to study its effect on their cooperation. The study showed that when the third person was interdependent with the subjects in playing the game, the number

[15]Anatol Rapoport and Carol Orwant, "Experimental Games: A Review," *Behavioral Science*, 7, No. 1 (1962), 15.

[16]Phillip S. Gallo, Jr., and Charles G. McClintock, "Cooperative and Competitive Behavior in Mixed-Motive Games," *Journal of Conflict Resolution*, 9, No. 1 (1965), 73.

[17]Reported in Gallo and McClintock, "Cooperative and Competitive Behavior," p. 74.

of trusting choices increased between the two. Their cooperation dropped if the "obnoxious" third party was only an observer, and it dropped again if he was not present.

The presence of a "common enemy" has been shown elsewhere to build internal group solidarity, cooperation, and cohesiveness.[18] Of course, this process contributes to tighter group boundaries, stereotyping, and hostility toward outgroups. The gains of cooperation at one level appear to be at the expense of cooperation at a broader level. Certainly, the experience of internal group cooperation and external group rivalry is a familiar process and a common problem in organizations. The presence of multiple competing interests suggests that cooperative behavior may be a finite quantity in organizations: More cooperation at one level means less at another. At any rate, this analysis of the trust dilemma has brought the discussion full circle to the problem of potentially conflicting loyalties in organizations.

The final section of this chapter explores the question of self and collective orientations from the position of the political leader or statesman. In part, this is the issue of power and responsibility.

Power and Responsibility

Dilemmas for leaders and members. Organizational leaders carry broad responsibility for the well-being of their organizations, and yet they are held accountable to specific groups with specific values and interests. A leader usually seeks personal survival and advancement and needs to maintain a basis of support, or constituency. And yet, constituency interests may not coincide with broad organizational interests that the leader, by virtue of his or her position, is also expected to seek. The two dimensions of institutional and personal interests can create a tension for leadership decision.

These two criteria of choice give rise to several dilemmas of power and responsibility. It is in the interest of the members of a government or organization to give a leader discretion and latitude. Leaders need flexibility to act in terms of broad interests. On the other hand, discretion and flexibility open the possibility for decisions that favor personal interests of the leader rather than the broad interests of the system. While discretion creates opportunities for statesmanship, it also affords the risk of self-aggrandizement at the expense of the institution. The abuse of

---

[18]Muzafer Sherif, "Experiments in Group Conflict and Co-operation," in *Readings in Managerial Psychology*, eds. Harold J. Leavitt and Louis R. Pondy (Chicago: University of Chicago Press, 1964).

power was one of the articles of impeachment debated and passed by the House of Representatives Judiciary Committee in its investigation of Richard Nixon's performance in the office of the presidency.

The leader also faces a dilemma: One may want to act on institutional needs, but not at the expense of undercutting his or her own career. What are reasonable private interests to pursue, and to what extent can they be pursued without jeopardizing the organizational or the public interests? What degree of self-restraint is it reasonable to expect of oneself in administration?

A leader also expects others to pursue special interests, but to maintain a level of self-restraint in the interest of a larger welfare. The leader's own view of this issue influences the "rules of the game" within a certain latitude and is a factor in the morale and horizons of members. One person suggests that this intangible attitude is one of the primary responsibilities and consequences of successful leadership.[19] A climate for others' decisions emanates from the leader's own style and philosophy.

Probably the most notable example of a national leader holding to an integrationist ideology is Woodrow Wilson.[20] First in relation to internal political processes and later in the context of world affairs, Wilson sought to realize a harmonious community of interests. He viewed human nature as seeking peace, freedom, and justice. The interests of individuals and communities, he thought, are brought together by eliminating injustices that are the consequence of materialistic and ambitious desires. Individuals can and will, with the encouragement of national leaders, exercise enlightened self-interest and relate their own interest to the community well-being.

Wilson was unsuccessful in his attempts to make the League of Nations an effective forum for resolution of international conflicts. This failure attests to the fact that social systems are political systems, and political processes cannot be ignored. However, the relative emphasis on unity or special interests is a matter of choice.

Political leadership. The tension between partisanship and national interest in the lives of political figures in the United States was examined in John F. Kennedy's book, *Profiles in Courage*.[21] This study illustrated some outstanding examples of U.S. senators who, at various times throughout the country's history, acted in terms of national rather than private

---

[19]Chester I. Barnard, *The Functions of the Executive* (Cambridge, Mass.: Harvard University Press, 1938), Chap. XVII.

[20]See, for example, Harry Clor, "Woodrow Wilson," in *American Political Thought*, eds. Morton J. Frisch and Richard G. Stevens (New York: Scribner's, 1971).

[21]John F. Kennedy, *Profiles in Courage* (New York: Harper & Row, 1964).

interests. Although Kennedy was aware of the common criteria of personal ambition and party and sectional loyalties, he also saw personal conscience and national welfare as criteria for actions by senators. His study particularly illustrates the tension between a leader's political requirement for popularity, usually gained by representing a constituency, and a leader's desire to pursue general, and occasionally unpopular, values.

One of the people described in *Profiles in Courage* is George W. Norris, senator from Nebraska for forty years. While Norris's role in the development of the concept of public power, and especially the Tennessee Valley Authority, is not detailed in Kennedy's treatment, his actions in this area stand as an outstanding example of the choice between collective and local values.

Norris was the foremost public figure throughout the 1920s defending and expounding the concept of public power, and for much of this time he was nearly the sole advocate of this movement.[22] The point of greatest specific controversy was the government's disposition or retention of the war-related power and manufacturing facilities at Muscle Shoals, Alabama. For more than a decade, Norris's persuasive ability and legislative skill prevented Muscle Shoals, the forerunner of the TVA, from being sold to private concerns. At the same time, his efforts to create a government agency built around Muscle Shoals to provide for flood control, navigation, and power development in the Tennessee River Valley were blocked by presidential action.

Controversy swirled on this issue from the end of World War I, when the question of the ownership of Muscle Shoals arose, until 1933, when the TVA Act was signed by President Roosevelt. The Tennessee Valley was a thousand miles from Nebraska. Southern members of Congress, especially from Alabama, fought for the sale of the properties to private power rather than public development. The representatives from the American Farm Bureau Federation advocated private ownership. The Nebraska state legislature had been convinced of the merits of private development and had urged Nebraska's delegation in Congress to support immediate passage of one of the proposals for private ownership at Muscle Shoals. Norris was the object of antagonism in the Tennessee River area by people who believed he was obstructing the way to cheaper fertilizers and land appreciation. Once, while he was visiting the government's properties, government officials were so worried about local sentiment against him that Norris was given a bodyguard.[23]

---

[22]See, for example, Alfred Lief, *Democracy's Norris: The Biography of a Lonely Crusade* (New York: Stackpole Sons, 1939).

[23]George W. Norris, *Fighting Liberal: The Autobiography of George W. Norris* (New York: Macmillan, 1945), p. 259.

Why would he undertake such a difficult and personal struggle? There appears no way in which Norris could have benefited politically or materially from his persistence in this unpopular cause. If anything, his personal interest lay in leading a less controversial, less demanding, and more relaxed life. Why did he continuously engage in what appeared to be uneven conflict? Early in the controversy, in 1924, he is reported to have said, "Somebody has to make these fights. I think I have made more of them than any other man and, as I look back over it sometimes, I wonder why I do it."[24]

It is fairly clear that Norris was acting on his vision of the national interest in power development, publicly owned in order to bring the advantages of low-cost electricity generation to all Americans. His goals were to raise human and economic standards through power development, to conserve natural resources through land reclamation and reforestation, and to protect property through flood control. These values, he believed, were important features for all Americans that he did not see forthcoming within the existing arrangement of power control.

Norris's role in the development of public power is the type of act Kennedy refers to as courage. What is the motive to act courageously? Kennedy sums up the reasons behind a choice made for the general welfare in the political sphere:

> . . . because each one's need to maintain his own respect for himself was more important to him than his popularity with others—because his desire to win or maintain a reputation for integrity and courage was stronger than his desire to maintain his office—because his conscience, his personal standard of ethics, his integrity or morality, call it what you will—was stronger than the pressures of public disapproval—because his faith that his course was the best one, and would ultimately be vindicated, outweighed his fear of public reprisal.[25]

The actions of public figures are more visible than the actions of people within everyday organizations, but the dilemma of organizational and private interests exists throughout administration. For example, one study of the impact of budgets on people in business organizations concluded that budgetary procedures encourage narrow departmental interests rather than fostering interdepartmental and plant-wide interests.[26] In this way, budgets that are set up to aid the organization's need for cost and production control may have the negative effect of encouraging parochial views. One factory supervisor in this study commented, "Each

[24]Lief, *Democracy's Norris*, p. 258.
[25]Kennedy, *Profiles*, pp. 209–10.
[26]Chris Argyris, "Human Problems with Budgets," *Harvard Business Review*, 31, No. 1 (1953), 97–110.

of us gets *his* own picture when we get the budget results. Even if we got the total picture, it wouldn't mean much to us . . . *we're primarily interested in our own department.*" While budgets may encourage narrow rather than broad interests, it is still the individual who holds an attitude and chooses the basis on which to act and to evaluate others' actions. In the final analysis, people, not budgets, make decisions.

Another example of this issue comes from Peter Blau's study of a state employment agency.[27] The agency's goal was to place the best-qualified persons in the jobs that were available; it also sought to emphasize counseling of applicants for training and occupational adjustments. Yet in actual practice, the first client with minimal qualifications was referred to a given job opening, and counseling was virtually nonexistent. In this case, incentives encouraged these narrow interests, since agency appropriations were based principally on the number of placements made.

Various organizational concepts exist that seek to align individual interests and broad organizational interests. For example, the Scanlon Plan is a system for returning to workers a share of the income from efficiency increases. At the managerial level, stock options and bonuses are mechanisms also attempting to bring together individual and organizational economic interests. Yet, regardless of whether a particular incentive incorporates organizational interests or not, each person exercises choice about what criteria are dominant in each particular situation. Structural incentives may alter the context of this choice, but they do not alleviate the necessity to choose.

The problem of ends and means. In modern organizations, as in all human affairs, power underlies action: Intentions have no force except when they are associated with a basis of power. Consequently, power is necessary in organizational affairs for the achievement of any ends a person may seek. At the same time, power implies importance, influence, and prestige for a leader, qualities that may be sought or may come to be appreciated in their own right. While one cannot deny these personal benefits of power, the need of organizations and other collectivities is for power to be exercised as a means rather than as an end. A major issue of leadership is that it may not always be so exercised. No one has written with greater insight into this problem than Niccolò Machiavelli.

Machiavelli holds a prominent place in the popular culture as a political realist. *The Prince* is an unabashed portrayal of the way in which a head of state achieves and maintains power. Machiavelli's prescriptions are strategic and opportunistic: He entreats leaders to place their security in the good intentions of no one, he recommends holding good faith and

[27]Peter M. Blau, *The Dynamics of Bureaucracy* (Chicago: University of Chicago Press, 1955).

loyalty in weak regard, he encourages deception regarding one's true intents and actions, and so forth. This side of Machiavelli is well known and, as a set of attitudinal and behavioral characteristics, has even been the focus of extensive psychological study.[28]

At a general level, Machiavelli is giving some simple guidelines: Effective leadership is flexible, sophisticated, and unsentimental. For example, he sees the need to be virtuous, but to do "evil" if the situation calls for it:

> Thus, it is well to seem merciful, faithful, humane, sincere, religious and also to be so; but you must have the mind so disposed that when it is needful to be otherwise you may be able to change to the opposite qualities.[29]

This is another way of saying that there are no absolutes in practical affairs. Self-interest appears to be ensured best by a relativistic perspective and an ability to judge the factors of each situation separately. Machiavelli states, ". . . it will be found that some things which seem virtues would, if followed, lead to one's ruin, and some others which appear vices result in one's greater security and well being."[30]

To a large extent, expediency and political opportunity are synonymous with Machiavelli. Yet this is not the whole point of his writing. There is implicit throughout most of *The Prince* a value placed on maintaining the unity and cohesiveness of the state. Machiavelli has a very specific purpose in mind toward which leadership is exercised: the aim of collective peace and unity. The value of maintaining general security supersedes the value of individual interests.

Machiavelli's own values are evident in the final chapter of *The Prince*, "Exhortation to Liberate Italy from the Barbarians." This chapter is essentially a plea to Lorenzo di Medici to lead the liberation and unification of Italy, at that time a divided and subjugated land. The precepts of *The Prince* are a technical guide and a bid to influence Lorenzo toward this nationalistic ideal. Machiavelli's philosophy is more a guide in the pursuit of a united and cohesive state than it is a plan for maximizing a person's political self-interest.

Of course, the same methods and techniques of leadership can be used in the pursuit of any number of goals. For example, it is said that Hitler kept a copy of *The Prince* at his bedside. In spite of Machiavelli's personal objective of Italian unification, the methods of *The Prince* may

[28]Richard Christie and Florence L. Geis, *Studies in Machiavellianism* (New York: Academic Press, 1970).
[29]Niccolo Machiavelli, *The Prince* and *The Discourses* (New York: Random House, Modern Library, 1950), p. 65.
[30]Machiavelli, *The Prince* and *The Discourses*, p. 57.

serve the purposes of any person or groups; perhaps judgments should also be placed on means. One needs to look beyond *The Prince* to *The Discourses* for Machiavelli's analysis of this danger and the need for the state to be protected from selfishly ambitious persons.

One of the themes developed in *The Discourses* is a concern that the ambitious not be allowed to corrupt and weaken the state. Machiavelli shows the need for institutional restraints on people's power, possibly safeguarding against the ambitious person's utilizing the tactics described in *The Prince*. For example, Machiavelli reasons:

> ... I say that a republic that has no distinguished citizens cannot be well governed; but, on the other hand, it is often the great influence of such distinguished citizens that is the cause of states being reduced to servitude. And to prevent this the institutions of the state should be so regulated that the influence of citizens shall be founded only upon such acts as are of benefit to the state, and not upon such as are injurious to the public interest or liberty.[31]

In this statement, Machiavelli warns against some who are capable of gaining power. Yet, by Machiavelli's own admission, a successful leader must be able to disguise true motivation, and it appears that he would have only those people read *The Prince* whose motivations are acceptable to his values. How is the "well-regulated republic" to discover the private nature of the citizen's true intent, if the citizen is an effective politician? The rhetoric of "the public interest" can be used and misused in the name of different motives.

Machiavelli illustrates with great admiration the selfless act of a Roman leader, Junius Brutus, who, after restoring Rome to liberty from tyranny, believed the destruction of his sons was necessary to insure Rome's liberty.[32] The difficulty is that Brutus was able to achieve power and to recover Roman liberty by feigning folly and gaining the intimacy of the tyrannical ruler. Thus, the recovery and maintenance of Rome's liberty in this example rested with Brutus's willingness to put collective interests above his family and personal interests. This would appear to be a vulnerable basis upon which to place the liberty of the Roman republic.

Self-interest and personal ambition can be both a service and a disservice to the general welfare. Self-interest is useful as a means of achieving power if a person's long-run intentions and actions are favorable to the overall needs of the collective enterprise. However, if a leader

31Machiavelli, *The Prince* and *The Discourses*, pp. 493–94.
32Machiavelli, *The Prince* and *The Discourses*, pp. 403–4.

fails to use the discretion of the position to enhance collective needs, self-interest becomes a strong disservice to the general welfare. With power comes responsibility. Yet the boundaries of responsibility to private and collective interests are usually not clearly defined, and the presence of both in a specific situation gives rise to a dilemma of administrative leadership.

CHAPTER REVIEW

This chapter has argued that managers face multiple and inevitably conflicting responsibilities, especially in the tension between responsibilities to themselves and responsibilities to an organization. The manager needs to be both an individualist and a collectivist. He or she needs to be able to foster the egocentric *and* to promote the collective welfare. At times, one must be able to place organizational interests second, and at other times, take actions that subordinate individual interests. The manager needs to be a disciple of Machiavelli in the narrow sense of making personal interests primary, and a proponent of Machiavelli in the broad sense of sacrificing private interests for the welfare of the whole. Organizations are comprised of special and private interests and of processes that rise above and integrate these interests; the manager is faced with fulfilling responsibilities at both levels.

Dilemmas arise in specific situations in which these responsibilities are placed in direct conflict. This may happen in positions of organizational leadership and create problems of power and responsibility, or between organizational units and involve processes of cooperation and competition. In interpersonal relationships, the problem takes the form of a dilemma of trust. No type of organization and no organizational member is immune to facing this conflict in some form; it is inherent in the nature of cooperative systems.

At the same time, the fulfillment of organizational interests is usually not left entirely in the hands of individual members. Most often, the central tasks and activities that need to be performed in order to meet organizational goals are specified through an authority structure or hierarchy. While hierarchy may be either a dominant or a secondary aspect of a large organization, it is inevitably present as a mechanism through which to achieve organizational goals established by high-echelon members.

Authority is itself a problem that contains conflicting forces: it is desirable simultaneously to control actions and to foster initiative, to direct people and to develop them, to centralize and to decentralize decision making. These and other problems, related to the interests of the collectivity become dilemmas of administration in their own right, and are the subject of the next chapter.

Chapter *3*

Organizational Control Versus Individual Development and Initiative

the problem of authority

The Central Algonkian Indians were a group of tribes, each consisting of about 3,000 people, living in what is now the region of Wisconsin through Indiana. Detailed analysis of one tribe, the Fox Indians, has shown that this size of social organization was able to maintain itself ecologically, adjudicate internal conflicts, and conduct ceremony and government with absolutely no social or cultural concept of authority.[1] A Fox Indian had no understanding of supra- or subordination, no one was "higher" or "lower" than another person, and the commands of European hunters, explorers, and missionaries were meaningless. Specific belief systems and repetitive roles in a limited number of tribal activities combined to "manage" the affairs of the people without the presence of authoritative relations.

While the absence of subordination of one person to another may be an attractive aspect of Algonkian culture, the same culture was not conducive to large-scale organization and the mastery of complex tasks, such as territorial defense against colonists. In contrast, the European explorers and American settlers who eventually dominated the Algonkian Indians had a culture of strong authority relations that was also consistent with the coordination of a large number of specialized and technical activities. Hierarchical relations were a familiar aspect of the European culture that proved dominant over the Algonkian culture.

The comparison of the Algonkian Indians' tribal structure with hierarchical organization is not to suggest that the Indians had more dis-

[1]Walter B. Miller, "Two Concepts of Authority," *The American Anthropologist*, April 1955.

cretion and control of activities than have a number of contemporary organizations. The Fox Indians learned a series of activities to be conducted in tribal affairs. For any one person, these were highly homogeneous and unvarying—the activities of each member of the tribe were relatively stable over long periods. In addition, the Fox Indian belonged to only one organization, the tribe, and each member's activities comprised a single life role. Activities of managers in modern work organizations are generally not as homogeneous and stable as those of the Fox Indians, and an organizational role represents only limited, specialized aspects of one's life.

The Fox Indians had arrived at a successful integration of individual significance and group structure. Whereas this system offered a personal freedom by the absence of authoritative command, modern institutions may offer a different type of freedom through a greater variety of roles, tasks, and skills. The comparison of Algonkian organization and contemporary formal organization attempts to show that regulation is an essential aspect of organization in any culture. Some basis for regulation must exist, otherwise activities would fail to be coordinated and related, and organization would not be developed and maintained. The choice is not between control and no control. Rather, it is a question of the nature and distribution of control in specific situations.

Hierarchy, which is a consistent fact of contemporary formal organizations, is a mechanism of control in doing large and complex tasks. One of the requirements of modern organization is the direction, coordination, and control of numerous and specialized activities. Maintaining an authoritative relation between positions, roles, and people is a method through which diverse activities are related to each other and operational tasks are related to general objectives.

The role of supervisor is the embodiment of organizational control, since a hierarchy is simply a chain of supervisor/subordinate relationships through which direction and control of activities take place. However, there are two major complications to this simple idea in administrative behavior. The first of these is that people at each level of organization may seek greater control of decisions in order to better define and execute their work, and in order to increase their feelings of responsibility, interest, and challenge in their jobs. Work is simply more fulfilling as discretion increases. These desires for control of work lead to the question of whether individual needs for self-control and organizational requirements for direction can be integrated. To what extent can the outcomes of individual self-control coincide with the outcomes of hierarchical control?

A second major complication to a simple view of hierarchy and supervisory control is that human development is also a supervisory function. One's subordinates are not simply entities with static capabilities—people can and do learn, grow, and increase in their abilities in work, and an organization as a whole requires this type of development. This need calls for a supervisor to help, to teach, to counsel at times, in addition to directing and controlling at other times. To develop and to direct represent two approaches, or criteria of action, for a supervisor in any given personnel situation. These dual responsibilities, deriving from the administrator's role as authority, are central dimensions of the dilemma discussed in this chapter.

Management theory contains wide differences in the ways in which authority is analyzed. One leading view, Douglas McGregor's Theory X and Theory Y, provides a point of entry into the problems of integrating self-control and organizational goals and of combining the criteria of control and development.

However, the problem of authority in organizations is not only one of understanding the dilemma of control in intellectual terms. Views of authority frequently carry ideological and moralistic connotations—beliefs that authority is inherently good or inherently evil. This dilemma is especially susceptible, therefore, to strong personal feelings about the rightness or wrongness of authoritative control. Several positions concerning the use of authority are presented in this chapter, and several responses to authority are traced in comparing two examples of program administration.

Two additional facets of authority in organizations are relevant to this chapter. The first is a question of freedom and order. Administrative actions, since they are based on authoritative command, necessarily restrict individual freedom. The definition of an "acceptable" individual–organizational relationship is an important issue in modern organizations and a focus of this chapter.

The second is the problem of control in terms of organization structure, usually considered as a question of centralization versus decentralization. While organizations are centrally coordinated and controlled, they also depend on the initiative and responsibility of people throughout. Centralization is valued for its contribution to planned and coordinated policy and direction, and decentralization is valued for its contribution to initiative and innovation. This chapter concludes with Bertrand Russell's theoretical statement of this problem and with Alfred P. Sloan's practical solution to it.

The Tasks of Supervision

Theory X and Theory Y.   As much as any other concept of applied behavioral science, Douglas McGregor's Theory X and Theory Y has captured the interest and imagination of administrators.[2] The logic of McGregor's theory might be described as follows:

1. The degree to which the jobs of a subordinate or group of subordinates are challenging and interesting for them is to a large extent a function of the assumptions held by the supervisor or group leader. A leader holding pejorative assumptions about people (Theory X)—that they are generally lazy and indolent, need to be directed and controlled, and do not like work—will act to restrict responsibilities and will exercise close supervision and strong control over subordinates. A leader holding positive assumptions about people (Theory Y) acts less restrictively and thus creates or allows jobs to be more challenging and interesting.
2. The behavior of subordinates is a function of their work experience. People thwarted in the fulfillment of needs for esteem, autonomy, challenge, and achievement become apathetic, dissatisfied, and antagonistic in an environment based on Theory X assumptions. In an environment based on Theory Y assumptions, on the other hand, behavior becomes more responsible, self-directing, and cooperative.

The behavior of subordinates is a function of their work experience, and their work experience is a function of the manager's assumptions and actions. In other words, the supervisor's assumptions and actions are part of the subordinates' behavior. McGregor's view is that motivation is inherent within the person—the manager's impact is either to enlarge or reduce the *opportunities* for this inherent motivation to be expressed. The role of authority is to create conditions in which "the individual can achieve his goals *best* by directing his efforts toward the success of the organization."[3] This integrative condition is possible only as organizational leadership promotes and draws upon the inherent ability of people for self-direction and self-control.

Contained within McGregor's view is also an example of the incisive phrase attributed to W.I. Thomas: "If men define situations as real, they are real in their consequences."[4] Assumptions about a subordinate's motivations and skills by a manager, even though they may be partially or wholly untrue initially, have highly significant consequences. This is a quality of self-fulfilling prophecy in the exercise of authority: Situations invalidly defined initially may lead to behavior that validates the original misconception. This process works to the disadvantage of subordinates when people are assumed to be less motivated or capable than they actually are, or to the advantage of subordinates when they are assumed to be more motivated or capable than they are and they rise to meet these expectations.

[2]Douglas McGregor, *The Human Side of Enterprise* (New York: McGraw-Hill, 1960).
[3]McGregor, *The Human Side*, p. 55.
[4]Robert K. Merton, *Social Theory and Social Structure* (New York: Free Press, 1957), p. 421.

Although McGregor does not discuss it, there is a corollary implication of his theory: The assumptions of a subordinate about a supervisor may also be self-fulfilling—that is, may lead the subordinate to act in ways that influence the supervisor to fulfill these initial assumptions. Thus, a subordinate who expects a supervisor to be highly controlling and authoritarian may avoid contact or fail to communicate fully, so that the supervisor feels a need to become more and more controlling. Or a subordinate who expects to be given extensive self-control and discretion may keep a supervisor fully informed on work progress and take full job responsibilities, leading the supervisor to feel little need for control and to be less directive.

McGregor's view, and associated nonauthoritarian perspectives in the behavioral sciences, have stirred not only interest but also controversy. McGregor is easily distorted; where he implies that external direction and control *are not the only* sources of influence available to a leader, he is often read as asserting they *are not legitimate* sources of influence for a leader. In addition, it has been argued that needs for self-direction, esteem, and autonomy are not important to everyone and probably not as important in general as they are to the authors of the theories. McGregor would not only accept the point that people do, in fact, differ significantly, but would insist that their differences, especially where people are capable and desirous of self-direction and self-control, have not been clearly acknowledged in administrative practice. McGregor implies that the general tendency is to err on the side of underestimating people's potentials rather than on the side of overestimating them.

McGregor's writing is readily interpreted as stating do's and don'ts of leadership: Theory Y assumptions are good, Theory X assumptions are bad. While he may not have intended this implication, it is easily inferred from his writing. Others have argued that McGregor was really proposing an attitude of inquiry. Administrators need to recognize that sometimes one set of assumptions is valid, sometimes another; the important process is to inquire into the specific situation. An administrator needs to be aware of (1) one's assumptions, and (2) the role of one's actions in a subordinate's behavior.

The leadership dilemmas.   Theory Y proposes a look at *possibilities* of the distribution of control between a supervisor and a subordinate. Supervisors, on the other hand, are faced with *realities* of immediate job responsibilities. Although a supervisor may want, in the long run, to exercise only general control and direction, the problem is one of ensuring successful and timely completion of day-to-day work. A supervisor's appraisal that the present work will not be satisfactorily completed in the absence of close direction and control may be accurate. Subordinates may not, because of natural qualities or ingrained experience, seek or accept increased initiative, responsibility, and self-control. A revised distribution of control is by no means an automatic success, and may be expensive in terms of lowering work output. In addition, although a subordinate's sense of responsibility and commitment may be increased by greater discretion and self-control, it may also be true that such discretion could lead to actions inimical to the goals of the organization. The question for a supervisor is whether exercising only general control may result in serious deviations from, rather than improvements in, the attainment of organizational objectives. The choice between an existing situation that is certain and a possibly improved or possibly worsened situation that is uncertain presents an administrative dilemma.

Another point concerns McGregor's observation that behavior can be influenced and developed through appropriate managerial assumptions and actions. Development of human resources is a central supervisory responsibility, essential for the long-run maintenance and growth of the organization. A supervisor's role is not simply to direct, coordinate, and control—it is also to train, to counsel, to assist subordinates in expanding their job capabilities and skills. One aspect of authority is to create the opportunities and bring the resources to bear that will release individual potentialities to the benefit of organization and person. This dimension of leadership first asks where the individual wants and needs to grow. It fully accepts the person at his or her present level of ability and performance and fosters a facilitative process in line with the person's own direction.

As a supervisor pursues specific work, explicit direction and control are often appropriate processes, but as he or she pursues subordinate development, counseling and assisting are more appropriate. A supervisor may frequently be faced with situations to which both these processes are relevant. In advancing the quality and/or quantity of work performance, overt control and human development are both valid approaches. Yet the orientations of giving direction and giving counsel may lead one to different and mutually exclusive actions in the immediate situation. In these circumstances, a supervisor faces another administrative dilemma.

A final issue may arise as a manager considers attempting to promote a subordinate's job development. Generally, there is the possibility that a person will develop a necessary level of performance if given appropriate learning experiences—for example, an intensive goal-setting process accompanied by feedback, discussion, and planning. But it is also possible that after a great deal of supervisory effort and energy and a variety of special training experiences, this person, through a lack of either interest or aptitude, does not attain the necessary level of work performance. If the person is not going to succeed in the long run, it is best for both to part company at the start. The decision to terminate or transfer becomes more, rather than less, difficult after commitment and effort toward development. Yet the eventual degree of success of the learning opportunities is unknown at the start. There are no *a priori* criteria available to a leader, and the situation calls for a personal choice.

The appropriate degree of supervisory control in organizations is an issue widely considered in the study of administrative behavior. Douglas McGregor's views offer a unique and clear starting point from which to explore leadership functions of the direction and the development of subordinates. It has been argued that these functions have various dimensions that can be in conflict and give rise to dilemmas of leadership behavior.

While discussing authority from a theoretical standpoint is important, dealing with the issues of authority in actual situations is often complicated by various ideological and moralistic reactions to the presence or the absence of authoritative control. We now turn to a discussion of the nature of predispositions toward authority and an illustration of their relevance to administration.

Authority and Ideology

Since questions of authority and control lie at the core of social organization, they are central concerns in social theory and political ideology. There are many points of view in these fields about the proper role of authority, from an exclusive emphasis on central control to an exclusive emphasis on individual freedom. For example, Thomas Hobbes believed that the natural passions of human nature, such as partiality, pride, and revenge, lead to social disruption and war unless constrained by a visible power that keeps them in awe.[5] Authority, by the fear of punishment, leads people to practice such virtues as justice, equity, and mercy.[6] At the other philosophical extreme lies the position of anarchism, which holds individual freedom as the supreme value. One author outlines its basic premise: "The essence of anarchist thought is the emphasis on the freedom of the individual, leading to the denial and condemnation of any authority which hinders his free and full development. . . ."[7]

These extreme emphases on the values of authority and freedom are

---

[5]Thomas Hobbes, *Leviathan* (London: A. Crooke, 1651; New York: Washington Square Press, 1964), p. 115.
[6]Hobbes, *Leviathan*, p. 115.
[7]D. Novak, "The Sources and Varieties of Anarchism," in *Patterns of Anarchy: A Collection of Writings on the Anarchist Tradition*, eds. Leonard I. Krimerman and Lewis Perry (Garden City, N.Y.: Anchor Books, 1966), p. 6.

reflected in management writing as well. For example, one author sees appropriate organization as a "benevolent autocracy."[8] This point of view assumes that subordinates are security-oriented and that supervisors have ingrained authoritarian approaches. Such complementary qualities between supervisors and subordinates encourage and promote the success of autocratic management. Most employees are unwilling or unable to contribute positively to the productive process, "there is nearly always a group of workers of indeterminate size who either dislike their work, have come without the expectation of producing . . . , or are chronically dissatisfied."[9]

These assumptions appear to be a modern institutional variation on the Hobbesian view of human nature as basically weak and needing to be "formed" appropriately by strong authority. In management thinking, this position sees "so many members of lower, middle, and even top management in the typical large business enterprises of today [as] dependent, insecure, and ineffective—productive only because they are bossed by one or two hard-driving strong autocrats."[10]

An opposing viewpoint also exists in the management literature. Chris Argyris, for example, views human nature as capable of and seeking psychological growth through work. Formal organizations unnecessarily hamper individual potential:

> We must conclude that the impact of directive leadership upon the subordinates is similar to that which the formal organization has upon the subordinate. Pressure-oriented directive leadership "compounds the felony" that the formal organization commits every minute of every hour of the day and every day of the year. Authoritarian leadership reinforces and perpetuates the "damage" created by the organizational structure.[11]

The proper solution to the individual/organizational conflict in this analysis lies in less controlling, directive, authoritarian leadership. While these and other positions are often located within the field of management science and management behavior, they do appear to have strong ideological overtones.

Predispositions toward authority. Attitudes toward authority are matters of belief, value, and predisposition rather than objective fact:

[8]Robert N. McMurray, "The Case for Benevolent Autocracy," *Harvard Business Review*, 36, No. 1 (1958), 82–90.

[9]McMurray, "Benevolent Autocracy," p. 82.

[10]McMurray, "Benevolent Autocracy," p. 90.

[11]Chris Argyris, *Personality and Organization* (New York: Harper & Row, 1957), p. 130.

Hobbes is no more "correct" than is an anarchist; Theory Y assumptions are no more "right" than are Theory X assumptions. In terms of actions, people also differ in the things they do or do not do in relation to authority. Predispositions toward authority are a central dimension of behavior in organizations.

Following World War II, the predisposition toward authority was the subject of intensive investigation, an account of which was published in the widely known volume, *The Authoritarian Personality*.[12] A series of investigations sought to explain the presence of ethnocentrism, fascism, and authoritarianism in human personalities. The authoritarian personality was eventually seen to be a constellation of attitudes such as:

> Conventionalism: rigid adherence to conventional, middle-class values
> Authoritarian submission: submissive, uncritical attitude toward idealized moral authorities of the ingroup
> Authoritarian aggression: tendency to be on the lookout for, and to condemn, reject, and punish people who violate conventional values[13]

A democratic orientation is usually considered the opposite pole of an authoritarian attitude. Yet there is another very real orientation toward authority that is neither democratic nor authoritarian. This is an antiauthoritarian predisposition. If the authoritarian is generally uncritically predisposed toward acceptance of authority, the antiauthoritarian is equally uncritically and moralistically opposed to authority. The emotional reaction is similar, only it takes the form of opposition rather than acceptance. An antiauthoritarian rejects hierarchy and structure as much as the authoritarian rejects unconventionalism. In terms of administrative leadership, the authoritarian is apt to consistently invoke reliance on order and structure at the expense of individual freedom and rights, while the antiauthoritarian is likely to consistently abdicate responsibilities of leadership and to avoid the structures that are essential elements of organizational survival.

Two examples of the presence of authority in program administration. What specific differences do the various ways of exercising authority make in the outcomes of organizations? The contrast of two examples of program administration, where a key administrative difference was the way in which authority was exercised, serves as an illustration of the con-

---

[12]T.W. Adorno, Else Frenkel-Brunswik, Daniel J. Levinson, and R. Nevitt Sanford, *The Authoritarian Personality* (New York: Norton, 1969).
[13]Adorno et al., *The Authoritarian Personality*, p. 228.

sequences of leadership.[14] One program was a leadership development program in the public sector, the second a privately sponsored administrative assistance program to foreign governments. Although they were in different fields, the two programs were very close in size and were both personnel development programs. Moreover, both directors had major responsibilities for participant recruitment, selection, and placement. For the purpose of this analysis, it is important to see how each director exercised the authority of his office.

The director of the first, a career development program for health professionals seeking to enter health services administration, was strongly "humanistic" in value orientation. He aspired to (1) provide efficient and thorough administrative support to those in training, and (2) to encourage individualized and self-directed training plans. He valued the personal development of each participant and saw his role as provider of a supportive, facilitative, consultative leadership with respect to each person's training activities. He tended to de-emphasize his role in determining the activities of participants. The experiences of program participants were varied: Some benefited immensely from the program, some appeared to be much less able or motivated to take advantage of its opportunities than expected, and a number had unchallenging training programs. The program had mixed results in terms of overall organizational performance.

The program director was proud of having an unorthodox program that pursued individual growth and self-responsibility. He clearly felt that the possible gains from "tightening up" the program in terms of administrative control and supervision of activities were not worth the potential sacrifice of program values of individualization and self-direction. The director was faced with an apparent dilemma of using the authority of his office to promote the greatest opportunity for individual responsibility or to contain and reduce the degree of nonproductive activity. He felt both responsibilities, which would lead him in opposite directions. Did he face an irreconcilable dilemma that implied the sacrifice of one value to the other?

The second program, useful for the purpose of comparison, was of comparable size and sought to place administrators in overseas adminis-

---

[14]The first study was conducted under contract with the Department of Health, Education and Welfare, contract number HSM–110-72-266, of which the author was project director. The program under evaluation was titled, "The Career Development Program in Global Community Health." The second program was a technical assistance program funded by the Ford Foundation. The study of this program is contained in a final report to the foundation entitled, "The Structure and Process of Technical Assistance: A Study of Two MIT Programs in Africa and Latin America," by James A.F. Stoner, John D. Aram, and Irwin M. Rubin, in collaboration with Virginia G. Nyhart and Nina Rosoff.

trative assistance positions. In addition to providing assistance, this pogram also emphasized unusual and challenging career work experiences. A study of this program indicated that it was able to integrate a strong sense of individuality and self-responsibility and an unusually high level of benefit to participants as well as recipient organizations.

In this program, the administrator paid particular attention to recruiting and selecting people, ferreting out and defining jobs, and matching individuals and jobs. Through these activities, he was usually able to set compatible initial expectations for employees and employers and thereby provide the initial conditions for an integration of individuals and host organizations. No administrative control was considered effective to achieve high performance once the overseas assignment had been set; the person's self-direction and -responsibility were then the determining factors.

Both these leaders would probably endorse McGregor's precepts, yet they handled control and authority quite differently. While the director of the health leadership program attempted to create positive conditions for people to assume self-direction through an indirect leadership approach, the director of the technical assistance program appears to have been more specific and direct in establishing a structure that encouraged self-direction. The latter director's use of authority was never ambiguous: He clearly assumed responsibility for selection of people and jobs and their matching, and he clearly gave the individual responsibility for his own actions in the work assignment. The director of the health leadership program created a more ambiguous role for himself. He was never clearly responsible or not responsible for participants' activities and performance. His constant availability implied that he wanted to be consulted by program participants; hence, they were placed in an implicit dependency position, calling for either reliance on or rejection of the director. In this way, there was a continuing subtle presence of authority and the absence of unencumbered self-direction.

Both program directors would probably agree in terms of values and principles, but their differences in operational leadership signify the difficulty in applying concepts dealing with authority. One major difference between their actions was the use or abdication of authority to structure initial conditions for participants that could enhance the opportunity for individuality. This selective use of authority in one program allowed the director to be accountable for the program and also to give independence to participants. Not acting to create as favorable initial expectations, the health leadership program director was less free to give independence to participants and experienced greater difficulty in reconciling his humanistic values with his responsibilities and accountability as program director.

In summary, the issue for administrative behavior requires a *non*-authoritarian rather than *pro*- or *anti*authoritarian attitude in organizational relationships. Nonauthoritarianism is removing the emotional connotations of authority and acting on the basis of descriptive facts of people and tasks. Mary Parker Follett defined this point of view as the "law of the situation":

> How can we avoid the two extremes: too great bossism in giving orders, and practically no orders given? . . . My solution is to depersonalize the giving of orders, to unite all concerned in a study of the situation, to discover the law of the situation and obey that.[15]

Freedom, Order, and the Psychological Contract

One of the key issues in social governance is the determination of the balance between freedom and order, between liberty and security. For example, to what extent ought a society to limit the expression of dissent in order to maintain stability? Or to what extent should disorder be risked in order to ensure individual rights? Different people are inclined to different sides of these questions. In the summer of 1973, this problem was discussed in the testimony of John Ehrlichman before the Senate Watergate Committee. The question was whether break-ins to obtain private records in psychiatric offices were justified in the name of national defense and security. Although Ehrlichman and others were later convicted of criminal acts in this regard, debate of the question brought forth varying opinions about such justification.

The tension between freedom and order exists as well in organizations. Does individual dissent and public criticism of one's organization strengthen or weaken the organization? What, if any, individual action needs to be restricted in the interest of the survival of the whole? People have honest differences in response to these issues.

These questions are usually resolved not in the abstract, but in the specific relationship accepted by individuals and by organizations as the condition of organizational membership. This relationship as a condition of membership has been termed, in literature of administration, a "psychological contract." This section discusses the concept of the psychological contract and shows its relevance to administration. We will also stress the fact that the psychological contract is vulnerable to misuse by either party.

[15]Mary Parker Follett, *Dynamic Administration: The Collected Papers of Mary Parker Follett*, eds. Henry C. Metcalf and L. Urwick (New York: Harper & Row, 1940), p. 58.

The psychological contract. The concept of psychological contract, coined by Levinson[16] and further developed by Schein,[17] is a useful way to view the relationship between individuals and organizations. In a psychological contract, the individual and the organization each have expectations of what is wanted from the other. For example, an organization may, through its explicit rules or more implicit norms, expect employees not to disclose certain information to outside agencies; it may expect people to refrain from stealing company property; it may expect constructive attitudes and a certain level of work performance of its members. The individual has expectations of the organization as well—for example, safe working conditions, a respect for individual privacy, liberal salary scales, or opportunities for learning and advancement—that are not written down or even, usually, clear and explicit. They are mostly informal expectations for the employment relationship. The joining of individual and organization occurs as each party feels that the other meets its basic expectations, and a mutually satisfactory contract is made. To the extent that expectations of either party are unfulfilled, dissatisfaction and conflict arise. There can, of course, be occasions when either party is exploitative. Organizations may fail to fulfill employees' expectations of a good employer, and people may take advantage of the flexibility, goodwill, or other positive aspects of an organization.

The prerogatives and limits of organizational authority are basic elements of any psychological contract between individual and organization. A mutual understanding, however implicit, of the rights and constraints of each party is a necessary condition for an employment relationship. The general nature of the contracts within an organization concretely defines the balance of freedom and order.

One may object to the notion that official authority of an organization is a matter of agreement among organizational members. It may seem more as though authoritative action is a "given" in any particular ongoing organization. This point was directly addressed by Chester Barnard, who stated that authority does not inherently exist in any person, position, or organization—that an action of one person toward another has authority only as the receiver of the action chooses to accept it as authoritative.[18] In *The Functions of the Executive*, Barnard wrote, ". . . the decision as to whether an order has authority or not lies with the persons to whom it is addressed, and does not reside in 'persons in au-

---

[16]H. Levinson, C. Price, K. Munden, H. Mandel, and C. Solley, *Men, Management and Mental Health* (Cambridge, Mass.: Harvard University Press, 1962).

[17]Edgar H. Schein, *Organizational Psychology*, 3rd ed. (Englewood Cliffs, N.J.: Prentice-Hall, 1972).

[18]Chester Barnard, *The Functions of the Executive* (Cambridge, Mass.: Harvard University Press, 1938).

thority' or those who issue these orders."[19] In other words, no one has control over another's actions, except as the other assents to control. Of course, the costs of not allowing control may be physically, materially, or mentally high, but the point is that ultimate control resides with the individual, and it is each individual's choice to give up or not give up control over any personal actions.

Obviously, decisions to accept or reject authority are not made for every act that occurs in organizational settings. Each person has a range in which actions of officials are seen as legitimate and are typically accepted. Barnard termed this area of legitimate authority the "zone of acceptance." Authority in organizations arises only as an action resides within this zone for a sufficient number of people: If no one in an organization accepts an action as authoritative, it simply has no authority. And, on the other hand, where organizational members have broad zones of acceptance, substantial control can be exercised in official roles.

The zone of acceptance, or the set of expectations of organizational and individual control, is an important dimension of the psychological contract. A supervisor and a subordinate may have different expectations of the extent to which commands require justification before they are executed, or they may have different expectations about the appropriateness of circumventing one another in organizational communications. Questions of control are frequently the substance of a mismatch of expectations between individuals and organizations.

In addition, the substance of the psychological contract or the zone of acceptance should not be perceived as static and unchanging. People may change their views of what is a legitimate zone of acceptance. Changes in this area occur as well as on the societal level; recent changes in society may be narrowing the general zone of acceptance between individuals and institutions. Examples of this point are practically everyday occurrences. For instance, in the area of employee relations, the Supreme Court has given a ruling that addresses the issue of the zone of acceptance between employer and employee. The Court decided that if an employee "reasonably" feels that an informal interrogation by an employer may result in disciplinary action, the employee has a right to have a union representative present, which can not be denied by the employer.[20] In other words, the employer cannot proceed with an "investigatory interview" without union representation if the employee has a reasonable belief that disciplinary action may result. To the extent that this ruling is an alteration of the relationship of employer and employee by limiting the actions of employers in this specific area, it represents a redefinition of the

[19]Barnard, *Functions*, p. 163.
[20]*Wall Street Journal*, February 20, 1975, p. 8.

psychological contract and a narrowing of the zone of acceptance in organizations. Through a number of relatively minor changes in formal and informal processes such as this, the basic relationship of individuals and organizations undergoes significant change.

Society as a whole is witnessing an increasing consciousness of individual and group rights that appears to be part of a general historical evolution of lessened dependence on absolute authority. Social attitudes in areas such as civil rights, welfare rights, rights of students in educational institutions, women's rights, and rights of professionals have been marked by conflict and controversy, if not by violence, in recent years. Challenge to existing authoritative action has been an area of social turbulence in religious, military, university, government, professional, athletic, and, to some extent, business organizations. In a variety of ways, a narrowing of the zone of acceptance between individuals and organizations appears evident. Officials, consumers, and members of organizations face the question, "What types and ranges of actions are to be accepted as legitimate authority?" As the zone of acceptance of authoritative action narrows over time, the nature of the psychological contract between individuals and organizations will continue to be an area of significant attention, change, and choice.

Dimensions of authority in a scientific study.   In 1963, social psychologist Stanley Milgrim conducted an experiment in which he placed volunteers in an intense conflict between the orders of an authoritative person, the experimenter, and the dictates of human conscience, that one should not seriously harm an innocent person.[21] Milgrim's experiment serves to raise two questions relevant to administrative behavior. First, in what ways can and do individuals and organizations exploit each other's constructive intentions? Second, could modern organizations potentially become highly autocratic and authoritarian relative to present-day practice?

Although the conditions of Milgrim's experiments have been varied widely in subsequent studies, the original study requested volunteers through the mail. Upon arriving at the laboratory, they were paid a small fee and were led to believe the experiment concerned the effect of punishment on learning. Each participant had a partner in the experiment who was to be the "learner." The "learner" was tied into a chair from which he could not escape unassisted, and electrodes were attached to his wrists.

The learning task was explained to be a series of word pairs. The learner was to indicate a correct word in response to the "teacher" by

[21]Stanley Milgrim, "Behavioral Study of Obedience," *Journal of Abnormal and Social Psychology*, 67, No. 4 (1963), 371–78.

pressing one of four switches that would light up quadrants in an answer box atop a shock generator. The shock generator was an apparently high-quality instrument with 30 lever positions in a horizontal line, each clearly marked every 15 volts, up to a total of 450. Groups of switches were also labeled, from Slight Shock up to Danger, Severe Shock, and XXX.

The experimenter told the volunteer/teacher to shock the learner each time a wrong response was given, and to move one level higher on the shock generator each time the learner gave a wrong answer. The goal was for the learner to learn successfully all word pairs on a list.

The volunteer read the word pairs and administered the increasing shocks. The learner did quite poorly, only choosing the correct term one-fourth of the time. The experiment proceeded on the basis until the twentieth shock was administered, at 300 volts. At this point, there was pounding on the wall from the learner's room.

During this course of events the volunteer/teacher could look to the experimenter for guidance, resisted continuing, or quit the experiment entirely. At any point of reluctance or questioning, the experimenter gave a sequence of increasingly strong responses, from "Please go on" to "You have no other choice, you *must* go on."

In the initial experiment by Milgrim of 40 males, 26 did "go on" to administer each incremental shock through 450 volts, even though no answers were given past the 300-volt shock. Most, but not all, volunteers showed extreme signs of tension and nervousness during the experiment and great relief at its conclusion.

The experiment was fake. The learner was a confederate in the experiment, and there was no shock given by the shock generator. However, the experiment had every suggestion of authenticity, and the deception was not perceived by the volunteers.

While there was wide variation between individuals—five (12½ percent) quit the experiment at the 300-volt point, and a few completed it without much visible sign of stress—most experienced great personal conflict in going beyond the point at which the learner ceased to respond. In this study, authority was exercised in ways that the subjects had not anticipated. The pattern of their reactions is a scientific matter and contributes, within the limits of the study, to knowledge about behavior. Yet this particular finding was obtained by misuse of the intentions of volunteers as well as violation of subjects' security and esteem. The questionable ethics of the study is a hotly debated issue: Is misuse of people justified in the name of science? How far is it appropriate for a person to use the esteem and authority given to the role of the scientist in a way that violates people's trust?

In administrative spheres, the same questions arise in relation to organizational, rather than scientific, purposes. For example, stress interviews tell a recruiter something about the behavior of a prospective employee, but is the potential disruption of the person's well-being justified by the need for this information? Some private organizations apparently conduct background investigations of potential executives routinely. Many organizations require psychological tests or interviews of applicants and extensive personal histories. Employees and potential employees may not be aware of the fact that the organization will ask for such procedures to be followed. And while organizations may not intentionally attempt to violate people's expectations, as Milgrim did, the question remains of whether some of these procedures do not misuse constructive intentions of prospective employees. Of course, the same problem of misuse can arise in the other direction. An organization's expectations for employee behavior may be overtly violated through acts such as stealing company property and embezzlement.

Finally, from the standpoint of the psychological contract, it is surprising that so many people followed the experimenter's orders with the likelihood of personal harm to the "learner." Obedience to authority prevailed over apparent risk to human life for a majority (65 percent) of the participants. Clearly, the mental "set" of volunteers was to be instructed and directed by the experimenter. Implicit expectations were not likely to include the possibility of conflict with the experimenter. The experiment perhaps best attests to the difficulty of revising one's set of expectations once under the pressure of the situation, and to the difficulty of directly challenging a person who is at that moment exercising authority. In terms of organizational behavior, this observation raises the question of the extent to which members might allow organizations to become autocratic and authoritarian if officials began to exercise control previously assumed to be outside the bounds of the psychological contract.

In summary, Milgrim's experiment raises two issues relevant to the present analysis of authority in organizations. First, the experiment shows that in the pursuit of scientific values, experimenters were willing to misuse people's intentions and goodwill. This fact has implications for the presence and exercise of authority in administration. A second issue concerns the conclusion that even the value of human life was largely insufficient to make people revise the implied psychological contract of the experiment and challenge its authority. This observation leads to the question of how malleable and open to violation are the zones of acceptance in organizations. In other words, how fragile is the present balance of freedom and order in today's institutions?

Control as a Structural Problem

In 1949, Bertrand Russell delivered a series of lectures on what he termed "one of the basic problems of our times," the relation of authority and the individual.[22] The central question of this address was, "How can we combine that degree of individual initiative necessary for progress with the degree of social cohesion necessary for survival?" Russell's concern was about the relation of individuals to society, and particularly, the proper domain of government. His question was how to ensure justice and security without creating authorities that restrict the liberty and diversity that are conditions of progress. "A healthy and progressive society," he stated, "requires both central control and individual and group initiative; without control there is anarchy, and without initiative there is stagnation."[23]

Russell was cautious about emphasizing order as the primary value of a society. He termed an "administrator's fallacy" the tendency to look at society as "a systematic whole, of a sort that is thought good if it is pleasant ... as a model of order."[24] The contribution of diverse and spontaneous attitudes and actions may be less evident to officials than is the value of planning and order. For Russell, it is in individuals, not in society as a whole, that the ultimate good is found: "A good society is a means to a good life for those who compose it. ..."[25]

Devolution is Russell's term to describe a government structure that best balances the needs for order and for liberty. The principle of this structure is that authority and responsibility are left to local organizations, groups, and people, wherever such delegation does not prevent more central bodies from fulfilling their functions. Of course, the proper functions of the central body in relation to local organizations can be a matter of debate. The balance between central authority and local autonomy was a major social innovation 200 years ago in the U.S. Constitution. The U.S. federal system has been a continuing experiment in the reconciliation of central and local control.

Large organizations are faced as well with overall needs for coordination and control, and with requirements for innovation and progress that come with diversity and initiative. The risks are that strong central control will foster stagnation and lack of innovation, and that a high degree of diversity will cause loss of direction.

One of the tasks of organizational leadership is to assess the balance of these two criteria and to seek their mutual influence. Rather than a workable integration, one often sees successive reorganizations over a period of years, first involving greater centralization to gain the values of central planning and administration, followed by increased decentralization to realize the merits of more localized administration.

[22]Bertrand Russell, *Authority and the Individual* (New York: Simon & Schuster, 1949).
[23]Russell, *Authority*, p. 54.
[24]Russell, *Authority*, p. 73.
[25]Russell, *Authority*, p. 73.

One of the apparently successful integrations of centralization and decentralization in business is the organizational structure at General Motors Corporation, conceived and led by Alfred P. Sloan. Sloan's thinking and actions have been well described in his memoirs.[26] In 1918, he was president of a subsidiary in a rather loose, almost anarchistic, confederation of companies known as General Motors. Becoming increasingly disconcerted with its sprawling, uncoordinated activities, he began drafting new organizational plans. In 1920, a series of conditions converged to put the company in severe crisis. Plant overcapacity and huge inventories had developed as a consequence of uncoordinated administration and lack of central planning. With an ensuing sharp decline in demand for cars and difficulty in raising capital, GM was put in a precarious financial position. Sloan's basic plan for organization was adopted at this time as a remedy to the ill-functioning of the company and has remained essentially intact since.

In memoirs of his career at General Motors, Sloan states that the essence of his organizational plan and, in fact, the essence of good management in general, rests on "a reconciliation of centralization and decentralization"[27] and the "right combination of freedom for the divisions and control over them."[28] His proposal for organizing the company was based on two principles: first, that the responsibilities and full initiative of each divisional executive "shall in no way be limited," and second, that certain central activities are "absolutely essential" to effective control of the company.[29] Is this not a contradiction of principles? It is, and Sloan saw it as such, but he also saw that in terms of effective organization, "its very contradiction is the crux of the matter."[30] The integration of these opposing criteria was attempted by placing responsibility for success or failure of a division with the divisional general managers, and by creating and maintaining executive and staff committees across the organization for overall planning, evaluation, and policy. It seemed that the spirit as well as the letter of dual responsibilities was developed, making this plan operationally feasible as well as theoretically attractive. Sloan wrote:

> From decentralization we get initiative, responsibility, development of personnel, decisions close to the facts, flexibility—in short, all the qualities necessary for an organization to adapt to new conditions.

[26]Alfred P. Sloan, Jr., *My Years with General Motors*, eds. John McDonald and Catharine Stevens (Garden City, N.Y.: Anchor Books, 1972).
[27]Sloan, *My Years*, p. 505.
[28]Sloan, *My Years*, p. 506.
[29]Sloan, *My Years*, p. 57.
[30]Sloan, *My Years*, p. 58.

From coordination we get efficiencies and economies. It must be apparent that coordinated decentralization is not an easy concept to apply. There is no hard and fast rule for sorting out the various responsibilities and the best way to assign them.[31]

This relationship of central control and divisional autonomy appears to have been an effective integration of opposites that created a successful organization at General Motors. Whether other organizations in business and other sectors can achieve such a well-balanced combination of centralization and decentralization is an open question. It is at least a certainty that large organizations do have these two criteria for structure, which often indicate different courses of action. It is the tension between them that often presents a dilemma of organization structure.

CHAPTER REVIEW

This discussion of authority in organizations has highlighted various dimensions of an administrator's role. No organization or society exists without regulation of individual activities. Even the Algonkian Indians, who had no concept of subordination, arrived at a highly regulated pattern of activities. In modern hierarchical organizations, a manager is necessarily in the role of authority. In the context of McGregor's leadership theory, we saw the manager as needing to make decisions about self-control, work output, and individual development. We saw the manager as both commander and counselor and possibly as needing to be both simultaneously. At the same time that the manager is involved in direction and development, it is also important to "depersonalize" these roles, a feat that is seldom an easy one in this potentially emotionally charged area.

As official and organization member, an administrator needs to be able to seek a zone of acceptance within a psychological contract that is a fair balance of freedom and order. The administrator also needs to be able to guard this balance from exploitation by other members.

Finally, the manager's role is to realize the degree of organizational structure and centralization that is necessary for survival, and at the same time to promote sufficient human diversity to ensure the progress of the organization. Just as progress cannot be secured in the absence of order, order soon becomes stagnation if it does not afford the freedom necessary for innovation. The administrator's responsibility is to both of these vital, and occasionally conflicting, criteria.

The preceding chapter focused on the administrative dilemma of individual and collective interests and responsibilities. The present chapter

---

[31] Sloan, *My Years*, p. 505.

presented the administrator as an official responsible for the achievement of collective or organizational goals. In addition to responsibilities of authority, the administrator carries other responsibilities deriving from an official role. Two of these are for efficiency in work and for equitable treatment between people; the former is an issue of economy and costs, the latter a problem of maintaining a sense of fairness in human relationships. To the extent that organizations are to be humane, administrators are also responsible for promoting processes of individual dignity and individuality. Situations to which efficiency and dignity, equity and individuality are relevant comprise the basis of the administrative dilemma discussed in the next chapter.

Chapter 4

Organizational and Personal Criteria in Administrative Decision Making

the tension between the rational and efficient and the humane

Formal organizations are constructions of logic. Work tasks, ideally, are logically structured and coordinated, and principles of logic specify and relate people's work roles. Day-to-day functioning in most organizations involves thousands of people and many thousands of tasks. The vast complexity of formal organizations is "managed" largely by application of logic to organizational processes.

Administration consists, in large part, of developing, sustaining, and improving the logical premises of organization. In administrative terms, efficiency is a major value that supports organizational logic, and efficiency is gained largely through the principles of standardization. Standardization is an operational concept that implies the elimination of technically unnecessary or idiosyncratic aspects of work.

Organizational logic, efficiency, and standardization are central elements of administrative process, and in the absence of other values, these elements would comprise the essence of administration. But organizations are not devoid of other and potentially conflicting values. Values of human dignity may, at points, conflict with the logic of standardization and the value of efficiency; the value of individuality may conflict at points with the logic of standardization or equity in handling people. The presence of organizational criteria on the one hand and human and personal criteria on the other constitutes a major dilemma of administrative decision.

Organizations require the performance of rationally designed sets of activities according to criteria of efficiency and equity. People who are called upon for this performance have individual habits, likes and dislikes, and needs for power, relatedness, and achievement—any of which may coincide with organizational criteria, may be irrelevant to them, or may conflict with them. Consider, for example, some situations where organizational or role criteria and personal criteria are in opposition:

> A plant manager is meeting with department heads to discuss a new manufacturing process to be installed in the plant. The present production design calls for a highly efficient and standardized process. One department head objects to the plan as impersonal and dehumanizing to the workers. This person suggests that the production process be altered to increase the amount of worker interaction. This suggestion is countered with the view that such changes will sacrifice needed efficiency. The plant manager sees this trade-off of economic and human values as genuine and ponders over the best decision.

> A nurse supervisor in a hospital is informed by the personnel office of the recent job application of a nurse with outstanding experience and recommendations. While the nurses on the supervisor's team are all competent workers, the new applicant appears truly exceptional. Working relationships on the team are friendly, and the nurses usually go out of their way to help the supervisor. To hire the new applicant would mean to relocate one of the present team members elsewhere in the hospital. The supervisor faces a decision of whether to place greater emphasis on strict work competence or on the loyalty established with the present work team.

> An agency director administers a public welfare program whose provisions a significant number of people have violated by receiving income while working. The director, responsible for prosecuting violators, feels that many but not all violations may have been due to ignorance of the law rather than intention. The director considers whether greater justice is done by granting immunity or by prosecuting all violators.

Each of these situations defines types of choices that people face in making evaluations and taking administrative action toward others. In each case, the manager confronts one criterion of an organizational value and another criterion of personal beliefs, feelings, and values. To what extent can or should the manager base a decision on other than organizational criteria, whether or not these criteria work to the special advantage or the special disadvantage of a person or a group?

Institutionally, all other factors being equal, efficient performance ought to be assured, the most competent workers ought to be employed, and violators of the law ought to be prosecuted. On the personal side, assuming all other factors equal, a humanly satisfying work environment ought to be sought, the social needs and loyalties of employees ought to be considered in work assignments, and peoples' intentions ought to be considered in judgments of them. However, a realistic view indicates that neither organizational nor personal interests are, or can be, pursued exclusively in administrative decisions. The question is not either/or but how an administrator decides to act in the unclear area in which neither standard alone prevails.

The dilemma of organizational and personal considerations is especially focused at points of evaluation and in decisions that clearly affect others. The issue is partly whether organizational criteria are waived because of the special needs of a person or because of the values or feelings of the decision maker. It can be argued that it is unjust to penalize an individual who has a special case in order to maintain organizational values and standard policies. On the other hand, it is important that administration be free of favoritism and inequities. Does not a waiver of policy for one person or group imply an injustice to another? Either waiving or not waiving policy requirements may violate one's sense of fairness.

The main issues of this chapter began to come to the fore in the early 1900s in this country, when the effects of industrialization had widely and strongly affected American life. Consequently, several of the significant social and management theorists of this time—Weber, Taylor, Cooley—provide useful perspectives on the dilemma of organizational and personal criteria in administration. Weber's discussion of a depersonalized bureaucracy serves as a starting point from which to view the logic and consequences of modern organizations. From it the chapter moves to other "classic" writers in organizational theory, contemporary social commentary, behavioral science research and theory, and even Melville's *Billy Budd*, in an attempt to delineate the nature and variations of this dilemma of choice in administration.

Organizations in Contemporary Society

Bureaucracy and depersonalization.   Max Weber's description of bureaucracy, written early in this century, stands today as the most comprehensive statement of the characteristics of formal organization. Weber's interest in the emergence of bureaucracy was broad and historical, and his definition of bureaucracy was extensive and detailed. He emphasized numerous characteristics of bureaucratic organization: for example, a hierarchy of offices, an appointed administrative staff, clearly defined areas of technical competence, and fixed monetary salaries. The aspect of bureaucracy of greatest interest in the present discussion is the perceived value of removing, as much as possible, personal factors and considerations from the operation of the organization. Personal relations are unpredictable and incapable of calculated decisions in administration.

The more bureaucracy can become impersonal, internally and vis-à-vis outside people, the more efficient and ideally functioning it is. Weber wrote:

> Fully developed bureaucracy operates in a special sense *sine ira ac studio* (without bias or favor). Its peculiar character and with it its appropriateness for capitalism is the more fully actualized the more bureaucracy "depersonalizes" itself; i.e., the more completely it succeeds in achieving that condition which is acclaimed as its peculiar virtue, viz., the exclusion of love, hatred, and every purely personal, especially irrational and incalculable, feeling from the execution of official tasks. In the place of the old-type ruler who is moved by sympathy, favor, grace and gratitude, modern culture requires for its sustaining external apparatus the emotionally detached, and hence rigorously "professional," expert; and the more complicated and the more specialized it is, the more it needs him.[1]

Weber was observing and interpreting the movement of Western societies away from a traditional base of authority in which obedience is given to a person within time-established traditions. He described society as moving toward a legal basis of authority in which obedience is given to an office within a legally established order. The need for impersonality is not an insignificant aspect of this movement, since traditional authority was based on a concept of personal loyalty. The "depersonalizing" of official relationships lies at the heart of the evolution of modern institutions or bureaucracies, and in Weber's view, large-scale organizations have no other choice than bureaucratization: "The choice is only that between bureaucracy and dilettantism in the field of administration."[2]

There is no conclusive evidence to indicate the degree to which American society has successfully depersonalized its organizational systems. Bureaucracies have clearly had an ability to grow, to the extent that a membership of tens of thousands is not uncommon, and such large-scale organizations appear to have an ability to sustain themselves at that level of size. If the development of bureaucracy requires the elimination of personal factors, as Weber declared, then wide-scale depersonalization of institutions currently exists.

But perhaps Weber was incorrect, and successful bureaucracy does not require such a high level of depersonalization. Or perhaps this requirement does hold, and our bureaucracies simply need not be as efficient for survival as they could be in an absolute sense. Perspectives on

---

[1] Max Rheinstein, ed., *Max Weber on Law in Economy and Society* (Cambridge, Mass.: Harvard University Press, 1954), p. 351.

[2] A.M. Henderson and Talcott Parsons, trans., *Max Weber: The Theory of Social and Economic Organization* (New York: Free Press, 1947), p. 337.

these issues can vary extensively and one is likely to arrive at universally accepted positions. It does appear evident, though, that personal forces can often be considered nonrational and illogical aspects of administrative decision, and it is probable that individuals' feelings will always be a factor in administrative decision making. The real question is whether personal criteria represent unjustified favoritism or defensible treatment of special cases. Also, the extent to which organizational and personal criteria are in the long run integrated is a more important question than whether individual feelings ought to be excluded from the domain of administration.

Societal implications. The lack of "humanness" of formal organizations has been a topic of social analysis and commentary from Weber's day until the present time. For example, sociologist Charles Cooley, also writing early in this century, discussed why social ideals such as freedom and unity that arise in "primary" groups of family, childhood fellowships, and neighborhood are not achieved on a larger scale—namely, in social institutions.[3] Cooley's response was that the element of increasing size prevents face-to-face interaction and inhibits the communication necessary for achieving these social ideals. He states, "If there is no means of working thought and sentiment into a whole by reciprocation, the unity of the group cannot be other than inert and unhuman."[4] In this view, much of what is inhuman in social institutions arises not from evil intentions but simply as a response to the excessive demands of institutional experience on mental and moral energy. Human beings are simply incapable of meeting the requirements of large, complex organizations for preservation of ideals of freedom and unity.

The effects of size are easily substantiated in the personal experiences of most people. In addition, empirical studies have on the whole indicated that an increase in the size of a group or organization is accompanied by decreasing group cohesiveness, lower member satisfaction, and a lower rate of organizational participation.[5] These results, along with the observation of a general movement in American society toward an increasing number and size of formal organizations,[6] suggests that Cooley's primary ideals are in fact far from realized in today's social institutions.

[3]Charles Horton Cooley, *Social Organization: A Study of the Larger Mind* (New York: Scribner's, 1909).
[4]Cooley, *Social Organization*, p. 54.
[5]Edwin J. Thomas and Clinton F. Fink, "Effects of Group Size," *Psychological Bulletin*, Vol. 60, No. 4 (1963), 371–84.
[6]Kenneth E. Boulding, *The Organizational Revolution* (New York: Harper & Row, 1953).

A more contemporary critique of the dehumanization of modern society comes from the mental health field. Bernard, Ottenberg, and Redl, mental health specialists, have analyzed the psychological process of dehumanization in general, and specifically in reference to the risk of nuclear war and extermination.[7] These authors perceive an increased demand upon people to adapt to a rapidly changing society—what in popular terms has been called "future shock." At the same time, they see a growing inability of people to incorporate new social aspects of "time, space, magnitude, speed, automation, distance and irreversibility" into human relationships. The anxiety arising from this bombardment of social change may lead to cutting oneself off from experience as an emotional self-defense. These authors define dehumanization as a "defense against painful or overwhelming emotion [that] entails a decrease in a person's sense of his own individuality and in his perception of the humanness of other people."[8] Dehumanization is an emotional protection that involves both a reduction in the fullness of one's feelings toward others and a weakened sense of self.

The mental health perspective, as put forth by Bernard et al., does not deny the functional aspect of emotional defenses. They acknowledge, consistent with Weber, the "professional" quality of emotional detachment and its contribution to helping one to adapt to the demands of institutional settings. Yet they are primarily concerned that the increased complexity and rate of change of society may depress the degree to which one's own individuality is experienced and the extent to which others are perceived as fully human—that is, capable of arousing conscience and empathy.

If this is accurate, such societal developments reinforce the impersonal standard of bureaucracy and thereby contribute to increased social alienation. In the face of possible societal pressures toward "dehumanization," social institutions need to encourage an increased sense of personal responsibility for the consequences of individual decisions. Increasing personal responsibility in the context of the present discussion is to raise the salience of the organizational/personal dilemma and to make clear and explicit the criteria of choices that affect others.

Kurt Vonnegut, through his figure Eliot Rosewater and Rosewater's science-fiction hero Kilgore Trout, offers a related social commentary.[9] Vonnegut's imagery extends a process of depersonalization to the extreme, where people feel "silly and pointless" and can apparently think

[7]Viola W. Bernard, Perry Ottenberg, and Fritz Redl, "Dehumanization," in *Sanctions for Evil*, eds. Nevitt Sanford and Craig Comstock (San Francisco: Jossey-Bass, 1971), pp. 102–24.

[8]Bernard, Ottenberg, and Redl, "Dehumanization," p. 102.

[9]Kurt Vonnegut Jr., *God Bless You, Mr. Rosewater* (New York: Dell, 1965).

of themselves and others only in instrumental terms. The setting in one of Trout's novels is a nearly completely automated America, in which three or more Ph.D. degrees are needed to get a job. All natural causes of death have been conquered and consequently, death is voluntary. One man, volunteering to ease the overpopulation problem, asks his death stewardess if he will go to heaven, and she says she thinks he will:

> He asked if he would see God, and she said, "Certainly, honey."
> And he said, "I sure hope so. I want to ask Him something I never was able to find out down here."
> "What's that?" she said, strapping him in.
> "What in hell are people *for?*"[10]

Organizations have purposes, fulfill social roles, and in part, relate to the solution of social problems. But will we have gained or lost more if, in the long run, social problems are solved through the efforts of organizations that require a depersonalization of human experience? As Vonnegut implies, what is the value of ultimately conquering all natural threats to life if, in pursuit of this and other goals, people lose their capacity to value experience and life as an end in itself?

Weber's reconsideration of bureaucracy. To Weber, the value of controlling and eliminating "noncalculable" behavior in organizations was in achieving greater bureaucratic efficiency. He saw bureaucratization as an inexorable, irresistible force of modern society. Yet Weber was not without reservations about the social consequences of the bureaucratized society, and he challenged an "unquestioning idolization of bureaucracy." In a debate in 1909, he stated his reservations on several grounds. Weber's comments that are relevant here concern the tendency for systematization and rationalization to narrow the individual's perspective and individuality.

> Already now, throughout private enterprise in wholesale manufacture, as well as in all other economic enterprises run on modern lines . . . rational calculation is manifest at every stage. By it, the performance of each individual worker is mathematically measured, each man becomes a little cog in the machine and, aware of this, his one preoccupation is whether he can become a bigger cog.
> . . . It is still more horrible to think that the world could one day be filled with nothing but these little cogs, little men clinging to little jobs and striving towards bigger ones. . . . This passion for bureaucracy . . . is enough to drive one to despair. It is as if in politics . . .

[10]Vonnegut, *Rosewater*, p. 21.

we were deliberately to become men who need "order" and nothing but order, who become nervous and cowardly if for one moment this order wavers, and helpless if they are torn away from their total incorporation in it. That the world should know no men but these: It is such an evolution that we are already caught up, and the great question is therefore not how we can promote and hasten it, but what can we oppose to this machinery in order to keep a portion of mankind free from this parcelling-out of the soul, from this supreme mastery of the bureaucratic way of life.[11]

Criticisms and suggestions for modifications of bureaucracy have arisen from the pens of social psychologists, political scientists, and sociologists. For example, either the theory or existence of bureaucracy has been identified as limiting individual fulfillment and organizational adaptation, innovation, and conflict. In addition, the efforts of numerous industrial sociologists and psychologists have attempted to determine empirically the degree of correspondence between job specialization and worker dissatisfaction. On the whole, we have increasingly come to understand the undesirable, dysfunctional outcomes of bureaucracy.

However, bureaucracy and its attendant standards are neither bad nor good, neither wholly desirable nor wholly undesirable. We have seen that bureaucracy is consistent with and supportive of industrialized society, but that it may introduce dehumanizing as well as constructive forces. One challenge of administration is to manage the tension between organizational rationality and human considerations, a tension that arises from the fact that bureaucracy is a logical, but not a social, ideal.

Economic and Human Considerations in Industrial Practice

Max Weber expressed a concern about the mathematical measurement of individual workers and about people becoming "cogs" in organizational machines. Any discussion of rationalization and measurement of work activities in industry leads to a consideration of scientific management, or what is generally known as time and methods engineering. This is one area in which economic and human values clashed severely in the industrial history of the United States.

Typically, the compromises, trade-offs, and integrations of economic and human criteria are made in partial and incomplete day-to-day decision processes. Rarely is a nation confronted with taking an explicit public position in a contest between these two criteria. However, this was

[11]J.P. Mayer, *Max Weber and German Politics: A Study in Political Sociology* (London: Faber & Faber, 1943), pp. 96 and 97.

the case in the early 1900s in the U.S. Congress, regarding the potential merits and abuses of scientific management, or the system of shop management known as Taylorism. The public debate over this issue offers insight into the historical considerations about work, and it may create a way of understanding more clearly the issues of today's social policy.

The widely known "Taylor system" was a set of principles for productivity improvement based on efficiency gains in manufacturing plants. Through "methods" studies, particularly time and motion studies and various forms of standardization, planning, and systemization of the laborer's work, productivity gains could be realized.

Frederic Winslow Taylor's belief was that reduction and elimination of inefficient movements and processes could result in *both* higher employee wages *and* a low labor cost per unit of production. For example, a familiar case cited by Taylor was the daily cost of production of a lathe.[12] Under the old system of day rates, a lathe operator earned $2.50 per day. The cost of running the machine was $3.37 for the day. Five pieces of product were being produced in this case, at a combined labor plus machine cost of $5.87 per day, or $1.17 per piece. Through efficiency studies, Taylor designed the work so that ten pieces could be produced instead of five. If the lathe operator succeeded in producing all ten, he was paid $3.50. This $3.50 labor cost plus $3.37 machine cost added up to $6.87 per day, but the cost per unit for 10 units was only 69 cents. By this logic, the employee would benefit through increased wages and the employer would benefit through reduced labor costs per unit.

An additional aspect of the Taylor system was the incentive payment to the operator. If the operator successfully completed all ten production pieces, $3.50, or 35 cents per piece, was paid. If not all were completed only $2.50, or 25 cents per piece, was paid. Thus, in Taylor's view, the laborer could not earn less than he did under the day rate, and he had the incentive of increasing the wage to $3.50.

Needless to say, the Taylor system was vigorously opposed by workmen and unions. It could well appear to them that their basic rate of pay was being reduced from 50 cents to 25 cents per piece, with an incentive of 10 cents per piece being added to the base rate. Thus, the distribution of productivity gains was questioned. Also, Taylor's logic was dependent on productivity gains from the elimination of wasted effort and "soldiering," or making a pretense of working. An opposing charge was that it required the working person to speed up the rate of work, to his mental and physical disadvantage. There were also numerous charges of perpetuating indignities and loss of respect to the working person as a result of time and motion studies. And since Taylor advocated studying

[12]Frederic Winslow Taylor, *Scientific Management* (New York: Harper & Row, 1947), p. 82.

and training people without regard to unions, his system could easily be perceived as antiunion. Finally, some criticism centered on the individual character of the methods and incentives, establishing a force toward competitiveness among laborers and the creation of disharmony in the work force.

The controversy broke into the sphere of public policy in 1911, when the House of Representatives appointed a special committee to investigate "The Taylor and Other Systems of Shop Management."[13] The issue was forced into public scrutiny because the U.S. government had been experimenting with and installing systems of scientific management at federal arsenals and navy yards. It had been "charged that this system is detrimental to the best interests of the Government service and to the workmen employed."[14] The special investigation was to review the federal experience with these new systems and to report its conclusions to Congress. Four months and 1,847 pages of testimony later, the committee's hearings drew to a close.

There was never any separate legislation passed to restrict the application of scientific management in national government service. The special House of Representatives committee recommended none, and a bill submitted to the U.S. Senate in 1912 by Senator Borah to prohibit the use of stopwatches and bonus systems of compensation in government work was never brought to a vote.[15] Later, though, as an indication of some of the sentiment against time studies, it became traditional to attach a rider to budget appropriations declaring to this effect and intent: "Not one dollar of this federal budget shall be expended to pay one government employee to take a time study of another government employee for the purpose of setting wage rates."[16]

The observations and conclusions of the special investigating committee of the House of Representatives are a useful study of an attempt to reconcile the opposing economic and human values raised by the application of scientific management. The committee struck a middle road, recommending to the House neither restrictions on the methods of scientific management nor the application of the system in its entirety in any government plant.[17] On the one hand, the committee endorsed the general objectives of scientific management:

[13]*Hearings before Special Committee of the House of Representatives to Investigate "The Taylor and Other Systems of Shop Management,"* under authority of H. Res. 90, 62d Cong. 1st. sess., August 21, 1911, Vol. I to III, 65851 UN 34T.

[14]*Hearings*, Vol. 1, p. 1.

[15]*Senate Reports*, 62d Cong. 2d sess., 1911–1912, Vol. 3, Report No. 930, "Systems of Shop Management," July 17, 1912.

[16]Personal communication, Prof. A.B. Cummins, Case Western Reserve University.

[17]*House Reports*, 62d Cong., 2d sess., 1911–1912, Vol. A-1, Report No. 403, "Taylor and Other Systems of Shop Management," March 9, 1912.

It appears to your committee that no one can seriously object, and as a matter of fact no one has objected, to any system which so standardizes and systematizes the work to be performed that a greater amount of production is secured with the same expenditure of labor.[18] . . . The Taylor system undertakes to standardize tools, machines, nuts, bolts, etc., so as to eliminate as far as possible the loss of time and waste energy resulting from the lack of standardization. This is a consummation devoutly to be wished.[19] . . . The elimination of unnecessary motion in doing any work is always a benefit, because it conserves the vitality of the workman and makes his labor more productive.[20]

On the other hand, the committee was attentive to the possible human costs of an unregulated system of scientific management:

A machine is an inanimate thing—it has no life, no brain, no sentiment, and no place in the social order. With a workman it is different. He is a living, moving, sentient, social being, he is entitled to all the rights, privileges, opportunities, and respectful consideration given to other men. He would be less than a man if he did not resent the introduction of any system which deals with him in the same way as a beast of burden or an inanimate machine.[21]

Efficiency must not be had at the cost of the men, women and children who labor and who should be the primary beneficiaries from efficiency. We should study how to produce that output and this must be done by conserving in every way not only their health and physical and nervous vigor, but by creating such conditions as will permit them to work out their own happiness and contentment, secure wages which will enable them to live in such a manner as to maintain their own self-respect, and sufficient leisure to enjoy the refreshing influence of mental and moral recreation.[22]

How to reconcile the values to economic organization of scientific management and the values of human dignity in the workplace? It was not proposed that these values were necessarily in conflict, but rather that human injustice might easily result from the management systems. What would exist to prevent these extremes of application? Proponents of Taylorism argued that the new management systems required a positive mental attitude on the part of the employer that would produce a spirit of fairness and cooperation with employees. In response to this, the

[18]*House Reports*, p. 2.
[19]*House Reports*, p. 4.
[20]*House Reports*, p. 5.
[21]*House Reports*, p. 3.
[22]*House Reports*, p. 2.

committee stated to the House, "Your committee is of the opinion that the mere mental attitude of the employer is too variable and unsubstantial a basis upon which to rest the material welfare of the wage worker."[23]

The committee appears to have realized that the value of scientific management was not a matter of either/or. It could not in the abstract accept or reject the new management principles, but implied that their value or disadvantage followed only from specific applications. Rather than reliance on a system of pay incentives to stimulate productive job activity, the committee stated, "the best and most effective stimulus that can be given to the work in a shop is to serve and hold a fine spirit of cooperation with the management on the part of the workmen." Such a spirit of cooperation was believed to be both a consequence and a cause of fair reconciliations of economic and human interests. This implies a certain level of mutual confidence, and as the committee stated, "Confidence is a plant of slow growth."[24]

In this consideration of the public controversy surrounding the "Taylor system," institutional interests were largely economic, and human interests concerned dignity and fairness to the working person. Although this specific debate on methods studies and other principles of scientific management has long since subsided, the issue of reconciling economic and human values remains active within the context of contemporary concepts such as industrial democracy and interests in the quality of work life. Each new phase of industrial development and change raises this issue in some form and seeks new resolutions and possible integrations of the inherent dilemma.

Just as the committee of the House of Representatives found it difficult to formulate a general policy in this regard, reconciliation of these values in the present day will occur largely through multiple, disjointed, and partial actions. The issues inevitably center on the choices and actions of separate individuals and organizations, facing specific and special circumstances. Thus, the criteria and processes of decision in these numerous situations of daily administration are central in an analysis of this dilemma of choice.

The Administrative Dilemma

The manager as an official and as a person.   As an official of an organization, a manager is responsible for both achieving the rationalization of work that was described by Weber, and gaining the efficiency of work

[23]*House Reports*, p. 4.
[24]*House Reports*, p. 2.

operations for which Taylor is a historical precedent. These responsibilities are inherent and basic elements of an administrative role. At the same time, the manager as a person has a responsibility to provide a human work environment for him/herself and others. Work rationalization and efficiency are not the sole criteria relevant to administrative decisions involving work organization. In fact, rational and economic values and human values can be experienced in direct conflict in this context. Weber's second thoughts about the impact of bureaucracy on people, and the reluctance of the special committee of the House to give blanket approval of the Taylor system, suggest that these observers sensed the tension between organizational and personal criteria and realized that the values of individuality and dignity are as legitimate criteria in administrative behavior as are values of logic and efficiency. The difference in these two sets of values is mainly that individuality and dignity are personal concerns, deriving from the administrator as a person, while logic and efficiency are values specific to the nature of organizations and derive from an administrator's official role.

Of course, not all efficient procedures are impersonal or dehumanizing, nor do humanistic processes necessarily lead to inefficient and illogical work structures. However, situations involving the trade-off of greater efficiency and greater humanization of work are real. Managers face situations in which both criteria are relevant and are in conflict.

A study of managerial conflict.   The behavior in situations of personal and organizational conflict has not been well studied. While there may be acceptance of this administrative dilemma at a general level of understanding, there is little knowledge of how human associations and organizational criteria are specifically related and how people deal with this conflict. An important step in this direction is a laboratory experiment conducted by John Humpel at the University of Chicago.[25] Although Humpel's experiment took place in the laboratory and is therefore a contrived situation, the reactions of people within the experiment were authentic and instructive to this chapter.

Humpel was interested in the existence of two "universal" norms in business: one of profit maximization, and the other of interpersonal reciprocity—the expectation that a person will help someone who has helped him or her in the past. Humpel identified a body of knowledge about each of these norms in the behavioral science literature, but the literature showed a lack of attention to people's behavior when the two norms were in conflict. Normative conflict was the focus of his study.

[25]John J. Humpel, "The Joint Occurrence of Norms in Business Organizations: A Study of Normative Conflict," doctoral dissertation abstract, University of Chicago, Graduate School of Business, 1973.

Humpel placed 192 male business students in an experiment of simulated management practice. Each subject was a "supervisor" in a two-person work team, the subject's partner being a confederate of the experimenter. Each "work team" was given a standard task with real, but nominal, monetary incentives. After working for a given period in which his partner (confederate) made a standardized performance, the "supervisor" was informed that he had a personal decision to make: He could choose to retain his present worker, or be assigned a new worker whose productivity was described as equal to, 10 percent better, 25 percent better, or 50 percent better than his present worker. The conflict of norms was between a personal criterion and an economic criterion: The personal element was the subject's desire to help a worker who had given help in the past; the economic element was his desire to achieve greater productivity.

While this decision was specific to the way in which Humpel designed his experiment, the situation has plausible parallels in actual organizations. The example of the nurse supervisor in the introduction to this chapter is a restatement of the structure of this experiment in a real-life context. In fact, Humpel's interest in this topic apparently originated as he observed company mergers in which managers were faced with a choice between continuing the employment of those with whom they had worked and replacing them with workers of higher ability from the merged company.

The results of this experiment showed that the personal criterion was virtually universal when the stranger was perceived as equal to the partner in productivity. In other words, "supervisors" almost unanimously chose their partners over strangers when no production differences were thought to exist. But when they were asked to choose between two strangers of differing productivity to play the game, without any personal association, they always chose the person of greater productivity. In the absence of other factors, economic and personal values appear to be universal.

Humpel also concluded that when both values are present, they exert opposing forces. For example, when a stranger offered a 50 percent increase in production, supervisors working face to face with their subordinates favored the partner over the stranger 41.7 percent of the time. Personal associations were a factor in their decisions, and the stronger the association, the greater its influence on the decisions.

Likewise, as the perceived productivity of the newcomer increased, the economic criterion of decisions became stronger. Including experimental conditions where the supervisors and partners did not work face to face with those where they did, as productive value of the stranger in relation to the partner went from equal to 10 percent better, to 25 percent better, to 50 percent better, the choices of the partner over the stranger went from 98 to 71 to 54 to 27 percent. An increasing economic value did compete with and did gradually override the personal value.

Specific qualities of an experiment such as this may not have an exact resemblance to actual administrative situations. For example, the consequences of a decision of this type in actual administration would probably be much greater than for a laboratory participant. The impact of the decision on an interpersonal relationship and the impact of greater productivity on the supervisor are likely in real life to be more consequential than they were in the experiment. The value of the experiment is more in identifying the structure of a decision that has strong intuitive parallels with actual events in organizations. This experiment identifies reciprocity, a powerful force in administration, as potentially in conflict with another powerful force in administration—the economic criterion. The participants in the experiment apparently found this a legitimate, if not a familiar, situation. This study may be a first step in the larger task of specifying real-life conflicts of these norms and ways in which people cope with them.

Equity as an Administrative Principle

If interpersonal reciprocity is a widely followed social norm that potentially conflicts with a norm of maximum production, the personal influence in reciprocity may also involve favoritism and may conflict with a principle of fairness. Most administrative situations involve more than two people, and a principle of equitable treatment between people requires the minimization of influence of likes, dislikes, and personal relationships. Why should one person's chance of receiving favorable or unfavorable treatment be influenced by the personal beliefs or values of a particular administrator and another's chances hindered by these factors? A concept of fairness demands universal standards.

The importance of equity in organizations has most often been seen as a question of motivation. Each person makes certain contributions to an organization in terms of time and effort, and each person receives certain benefits, such as pay and recognition. The principle of equity says that we all will compare our own balance of what we contribute to what we receive, with our perceptions of others' contributions and benefits. If we feel an inequity is being done to ourselves in this comparison, we are motivated primarily to decrease our contributions. If we feel overrewarded in this comparison, we tend to increase our contributions.[26]

[26]For a discussion of these points, see John B. Miner, *The Management Process* (New York: Macmillan, 1973).

Personal ties between people may often be a factor that create a felt inequity, as members compare their own contributions and benefits with those of others in their work setting. When personal factors become influential in some people's receiving special benefits of money, interesting work, recognition, or privileges, or influential in keeping standard benefits inaccessible to others, then feelings of inequity and charges of favoritism are bound to arise.

Sociologist Robert Merton has described the conflict between equity and personal treatment in the terms of the maintenance of stability in organizational relationships:

> The bureaucracy . . . is organized as a secondary, formal group. The normal responses involved in this organized network of social expectations are supported by affective attitudes of members of the group. Since the group is oriented toward secondary norms of impersonality, any failure to conform to these norms will arouse antagonism from those who have identified themselves with the legitimacy of these rules. Hence, the substitution of personal for impersonal treatment within the structure is met with widespread disapproval and is characterized by such epithets as graft, favoritism, nepotism, apple-polishing, etc.[27]

Individual actions in many administrative situations may seem to have insignificant ramifications if based on personal as well as institutional criteria, but many similar decisions in organizations have substantial implications. Personal criteria in decisions toward others tend to preserve inequality of opportunity that is often unfair to disadvantaged or minority-group personnel. Also, through exclusiveness of access, personal criteria may contribute to organizations' being unresponsive to clients and consumers. There is no possible way to determine where the nature of personal considerations or the frequency of decisions using personal criteria aggregate into a significant problem. The only clear rule is that one decision is as significant as any other, and each potential violation of the principle of equity weakens the social institution. A dilemma arises from the existence of the trust and distrust, liking and disliking, empathy and prejudice that are inevitably present in human interaction: Is it better to place fairness and equity above possible depersonalization, or is it preferable to act in terms of personal feelings and values at the risk of establishing and maintaining inequities?

Clearly, not all decisions and actions toward others are in the context of evaluation. However, dilemmas of organizational and personal values are a common aspect of decision situations, and thus an issue in

[27]Robert K. Merton, *Social Theory and Social Structure* (New York: Free Press, 1957), p. 204.

administrative behavior. On the one hand, personal justice is not served unless the whole person is taken into consideration. And yet, bypassing organizational rules and standard means of applying rules opens a wide area for discretion and judgment and thus offers the strong possibility of partial and inequitable decisions.

Individualized and personal criteria favor the goals of only some, and usually standardized policies and applications in one sense protect and in another sense act to the disadvantage of individuals. But the case is not clear—personal injustice may be and is done either way—and the administrative dilemma remains. In this case, how does one evaluate an administrative decision in a dilemma situation? There must be some way to conclude that one choice is, in fact, a better decision than another. This issue brings the discussion to a distinction between intentions and consequences in decision making.

Intent and Consequence in Administrative Decision

There is a natural tendency in administration to evaluate decisions according to their outcomes or consequences. Thus, certain decisions are "good" if their results satisfy criteria of efficiency, equity, individuality, and so forth. However, it has been argued in the previous sections of this chapter that these "outcome" criteria may often be in conflict with each other, and a "good" decision is not capable of being determined *a priori*. If this is the case, one's *intentions* in making a decision or in taking an action need to be brought into consideration. The ultimate evaluation of a decision may need to include what considerations or inputs went into the decision as well as what consequences it had.

The issue of whether actions ought to be judged in terms of the intentions of a person or simply in terms of the consequences of the act itself is a problem in ethical philosophy. For example, Kant's categorical imperative, act to always treat oneself and another as an end and never solely as a means, is ultimately a matter of intention. Allowing for intentions in administrative decisions implies that all criteria relevant to a situation may not be able to be satisfactorily met. For example, the performance of a person's work may be found satisfactory because of the person's effort, even if its outcome is less than desired.

The problem of judging intent or consequences where human and organizational criteria are in conflict was dramatically illustrated in Herman Melville's novel, *Billy Budd*. The story's central point is an administrative decision, in which to account for intentions is to base the decision on the human criterion and to judge only consequences is to use an institutional basis for the decision.

In *Billy Budd*, Budd strikes a fatal blow to the head of the ship's master-at-arms while in a fury of anger at being falsely accused of a theft.[28] A military court of three officers is called by Vere, the ship's captain and only witness to the blow. These jurors in Budd's trial are placed in the position of judging an act that is a capital crime according to the Articles of War, but that was committed by a person whom they like and trust, and with whom they sympathize. The jurors' predicament is stated by Vere: "How can we adjudge to summary and shameful death a fellow-creature innocent before God, and whom we feel to be so?"

Captain Vere knows instinctively that Budd was the innocent target of the master-at-arms' envy and false accusation. Yet he rejects consideration of human values in the trial—the injustice of taking Budd's life when believing he was falsely accused and thereby provoked. Rather, Vere insists that striking and killing a superior is a practical fact and "under martial law practically to be dealt with." Vere states the belief that even though military law may operate without pity, the individual officer's duty is to "adhere and administer it" without appeal to a broader "natural" law that prescribes death only for the guilty by intent. The officers of the jury are in a conflict between institutional and human criteria in judging Budd. Vere's attitude, expressed to the jurors, is not to "let warm hearts betray heads that should be cool."

The issues raised by Melville take various forms in administration: To what extent is a private conscience an appropriate criterion for decisions affecting others? To what degree ought people to feel personal responsibility for the fairness of institutional codes? And how far should empathy and understanding of intent be used as criteria for decisions that affect others? These issues are, to some degree, present in the performance of every administrative role. Captain Vere in Melville's novel is one who strictly separates his personal feelings, conscience, and belief in intentions from his administrative role. To some extent, this position simplifies the situation of choice, but whether it is a generally appropriate position is a question for each to answer for him or herself.

A Perspective on the Issue

As a final approach to dealing with the dilemma of this chapter, we turn to several writings in behavioral science that have touched upon the conflict between the official requirements of organizations and human or personal considerations in administration. For example, a statement of this problem by one author was expressed as a discrepancy "between the

[28]Herman Melville, *Billy Budd, Foretopman* (New York: Bantam, 1965).

pattern of expectations attaching to a given role and the pattern of need-dispositions characteristic of the incumbent of the role."[29] One variant of this conflict might be the organizational logic of impersonality, and the individual's desire for realization of personal sentiments in administration. Another perspective views people as holding multiple attitudes and outlooks, each of which is associated with a different role. Some roles become relevant to the same situation, yet cannot be simultaneously satisfied. One author states:

> In the words of William James, "As a man I pity you, but as an official I must show you no mercy; as a politician I regard him as an ally, but as a moralist I loathe him." In playing roles in different social worlds, one imputes different expectations to others whose differences cannot always be compromised.[30]

In these terms, a dilemma arises if one accepts the role of, say, "friend" and desires an action favorable to another, and if one accepts the role of "administrator" and desires objective standards and a personally neutral action.

One of the significant trends in the organizational literature of the last several decades has been the "humanistic" perspective. As much as any other single person in this field, Prof. Chris Argyris has devoted his writing to an analysis of the relationship of the individual and the organization and to the improvement of this relationship.

Argyris's position is that an incongruency exists between the needs of a mature personality and the demands of a formal organization: Whereas people seek a variety of tasks, a long time horizon, use of numerous skills, and psychological independence, organizations often require limited tasks, use of few skills, a short time horizon, and psychological dependency.[31] At middle and upper administrative levels, the incongruity of person and organization can be greatly alleviated and organizational effectiveness can be improved through improvement in the quality of interpersonal relationships. Openness, trust, and sharing emotions lead to improved decision making and, hence, to more adaptive and effective organizations.[32]

[29]Jacob W. Getzels, "Administration as a Social Process," in *The Planning of Change*, eds. Warren G. Bennis, Kenneth D. Benne, and Robert Chin (New York: Holt, Rinehart & Winston, 1961), p. 383.

[30]Tamotsu Shibutani, "Reference Groups as Perspectives," in *Classic Contributions to Social Psychology*, eds. Edwin P. Hollander and Raymond G. Hunt (New York: Oxford University Press, 1972), p. 68.

[31]Chris Argyris, *Personality and Organization* (New York: Harper & Row, 1957).

[32]Chris Argyris, *Integrating the Individual and the Organization* (New York: John Wiley, 1964).

Argyris emphasizes an aspect of the individual/organizational relationship that is different from the aspect stressed here. In the present context, the criteria used in deciding Billy Budd's guilt or innocence were the significant issues. The problem for the officers who were judging him was not that they lacked trust in him; their dilemma was created by the fact that they trusted and liked him a great deal. The issue was the extent to which they accounted for this trust in their decision affecting him.

One author, in particular, has developed a philosophy of leadership behavior that relates to dilemmas of organizational and personal criteria. Abraham Kaplan has written that "the leader must simultaneously do two things: he must be very, very close to you, and he must also be very far away from you."[33] That is, the administrator must have the ability to form close associations, to know and to allow him or herself to be known in relationships. He must have a security in closeness, not needing to avoid or escape intimacy. At the same time, he needs the ability to be independent—to not require such closeness at all times—and the security to stand the rejection of others if a judgment leads to action against their interests. The closeness is a subjectivity that is sensitive to personal considerations; the distance is an objectivity that accounts for the wider ramifications of decisions in terms of equity or economy, for example.

Kaplan discusses how the failure of some people to acknowledge and integrate these opposites leads to inadequacies of leadership:

> Some leaders try to deal with this dilemma by taking one of its horns and then the other in some irregular fashion, vacillating between the two in a way which is probably worse than resting on either. There is the leader who is entirely given to togetherness—"My door is always open," "We're all in the same position, boys," and so on.
>
> You also have the leader who lives in lonely grandeur. His is in splendid isolation, with countless barriers between him and those he is leading, and each of these barriers answers to a real need in him or in the organizational situation. A man in lonely grandeur can exploit this isolation in order to rely on his own judgment, to make the decisions, to be autonomous. But he pays the price in terms of the other major aspect of leadership, which requires that in some sense or other he represent the shared interests of the group as a whole.[34]

In an artificial closeness, the leader denies evaluative feelings to avoid the risk of standing independently and possibly alone. In creating

[33]Abraham Kaplan, "Power in Perspective," in *Power and Conflict in Organizations,* eds. Robert L. Kahn and Elsie Boulding (New York: Basic Books, 1964), p. 29.
[34]Kaplan, "Power in Perspective," p. 29.

an artificial distance, he or she avoids the risk of intimacy and of acknowledging the human consequences of actions. The first source of insecurity is an abdication of authority and weakens the institution; the second source of insecurity is an abdication of the relationship and has adverse consequences for people.

From this perspective, the question for administrators is not what they should decide, but how they can decide. Can I be secure enough to acknowledge my feelings on both sides of the issue? Can I maintain the patience necessary to postpone the immediate decision in order to look into the aspects of the situation, such as impact on the person and on the organization? If a leader can acknowledge the conflicting requirements and the opposing impulses and realize that the decision is dependent on the case, the rules, the context, and the consequences, then, in the long run, organizational *and* human criteria will be served.

Rather than adherence to organizational criteria or departure from them, the process of administrative decision involves leadership consciousness that reduces the distance between organizational rationality and personal interests. In the long run, what happens to the Billy Budds of modern organizations will not pose so much of a dilemma if the leader consciously takes the long view, and reorganizes, constructs, and integrates the organizational and personal factors germane to the decision. This is not simply "humanizing" the organization, it is meeting the executive responsibility necessary to maintain the vitality and validity of the organization itself.

CHAPTER REVIEW

This chapter has touched upon several facets of the relationship of personal and institutional criteria in administration. Max Weber's statement of the bureaucratic ideal poses a challenge to both administrators and theorists that continues to the present day: the extent to which logic or personal detachment can be, is, and ought to be sought by people in administrative roles. Organization size and rapid social change have been discussed as factors bearing on the problems of depersonalization, and social critics, including Weber himself, have displayed concern about the negative implications for people working in bureaucracies.

Just as Weber's logic of depersonalization represents a powerful criterion in administration, the logic of work efficiency of which Frederick Taylor was an advocate is also an important aspect of administrative decision. And just as the humanization of institutions is a counterpoint to the logic of bureaucracy, the advancement of individuality and dignity in work potentially conflicts with efficiency.

These forces press the manager to be both humanist and institutionalist, to be a passionate fellow human as well as a dispassionate official. In specific situations, they may place the administrator in a conflict between personal feelings, values, and loyalties, and values that rationalize and seek economy in work.

While personal considerations have merit in the process of decision, they present the danger of creating inequities if carried too far. As the manager needs to include individual and personal criteria in decisions without creating unfairness, he or she also needs to create human institutions without creating favoritism. The skill of the manager is to combine a high degree of closeness and a high degree of distance with people. It was also argued that effective decisions in this complex area need to account for intentions as well as the consequences of action.

This chapter and the preceding two chapters have focused on the relationship of individual interests and values to organizational needs for collective responsibility, central control, impersonality, efficiency, and equity. These chapters share the assumption that organizations can be treated as though they are concrete realities, and that the organizational values arising from this assumption are often administratively in conflict with aspects of individual needs in organizations. We now turn to two chapters dealing with the relationship of individuals to face-to-face groups. These chapters explore dilemmas of membership and leadership in relation to group norms.

Chapter 5

Individual and Group

a dilemma of individual preferences and group norms

Organizations are composed of groups in which the members often experience a "we" feeling. One element underlying group feeling is a group perception, or identity, such as "this is a hard working group," or "a competent group," or "a friendly group." A second element of a "we" feeling is the emergence of social norms—for example, uniform and stable patterns of dress, speech, viewpoint, and style of interacting. Group identity represents a psychological boundary of a group, and norms for behavior represent behavioral boundaries.

Norms for behavior, especially, create a basis for people to be members or nonmembers of a group. A person will not be psychologically a member of a group—a part of the "we" feeling—without some alignment of his/her actions with social expectations in the group. Norms provide a basis for group members to have different degrees of inclusion and centrality and for individual identity or self-concept. Some people's actions will be highly consistent with group norms, and the people will feel quite loyal to the group. Others' actions will conform less closely to norms, and they will feel less loyal to the group. The former are likely to be more central and influential in the group's affairs than the latter. In addition, those who are central to a group are likely to have potential social and emotional support from their roles in the group.

While forces for adherence to group norms are strong, there is often an opposing force in a person's desire for actions that run counter to group norms for behavior. Individuals may seek patterns of dress, speech, or working that happen to differ from social expectations in their group. The realization of personal preferences is often as strong a guiding force for behavior as are the advantages of membership, centrality, and support. The inevitable presence of groups in organizations raises the question for each member of whether existing norms are consistent with his or her preferences, and, if not, how to change the norms, adjust to them, or discover groups more consistent with one's own orientation.

This chapter seeks to explore the dilemma between group membership and personal independence in organizational settings. The basis of this dilemma lies in dual needs of the person—on the one hand, a desire for actions independent of social expectations, and on the other hand, a desire for close group association. The issue examined in this chapter is the nature of these opposing desires of people in organizational settings. What are the sources of norms in groups, what pressures exist for individuals in organizations between independence of actions and conformity, and how do people react to these pressures?

The resources for exploring these issues in academic disciplines, institutional practices, and literature are rich. The chapter begins with a description of how norms arise in interpersonal relationships and what purposes they serve people engaged in work activities. This discussion draws upon Muzafer Sherif's experiment on the pressures toward conformity, and Leon Festinger's analysis of the sources of uniformity of behavior in groups. Then we turn to examine the relationship of individual behavior to social membership—that is, what pressures can arise for individuals in relation to perceived group norms? This issue is first reviewed in terms of the small group experiments of Sherif, Asch, and Crutchfield, and then analyzed through the Irving Janis studies of institutional policy making. Also, a jury member's report of the group process of a jury deliberation highlights the problem of independence of individual judgment and social pressure. The final section of this chapter presents the actions and thoughts of several persons relevant to this theme: Some observations are gained from Albert Speer's memoirs concerning his involvement in the Third Reich, and some potential models for integrating group membership and independent action are seen in the examples of Dr. Stockmann in Ibsen's *A Public Enemy*, and of George Ball in the Johnson administration's Vietnam policy discussions.

How and Why Social Norms Arise

The autokinetic experiment.   In the 1930s, social psychologist Muzafer Sherif, undertaking experimental research on group dynamics, began with the common observation that human behavior is substantially regulated by social customs, standards, traditions, and laws—in short, by norms. His intent was to learn how group factors govern the formation of social norms.[1] To study this process, he designed an experimental condition free of external reference points, norms, or frames of reference. His first question was, What will individuals do in a situation void of standards of comparison? Will they be erratic and random in their perceptions, or will they establish their own consistent frames of reference?

To examine this question, Sherif drew upon a physical principle known as the autokinetic effect. In a completely darkened room where no objects are visible, a single, small point of light appears to move, and to move randomly. The movement of the light point occurs even when one knows that it is stationary, simply because there is nothing visible to which it can be related. The movement of the light point increases as its distance from the observer is greater, and as the size of the light is smaller. Sherif used this principle of autokinetic movement, first, to study whether people established stable judgments of the distance of light movement, and second, to study whether small groups of people similarly established stable perceptions, or norms, in judging the light's movement.

In his initial experiment, Sherif found that individual subjects did establish systems of judgment, and that they differed widely. The shortest median judgment of light movement for a subject was .36 inch for 100 decisions, and the longest was 9.62 inches; individual judgments ranged from 1¼ to 13 inches.[2] From his initial experiments, Sherif concluded that subjects "subjectively establish a range of extent and a point (a standard or norm) within that range which is peculiar to the individual, and that may differ from the range and point (standard or norm) established by other individuals."[3]

In general, it is useful to accept the result that we are able to—and in fact strive to—order or perceive our experience in terms of a frame of reference, and that subjective reference points are readily established. Second, the experiment distinctly illustrates how subjective reference systems vary widely between individuals. If one assumes that each of us has a sum of life experiences like no other single person's, then subjective reference systems are present and influential in the way people interact.

However, Sherif's conclusions with respect to individuals need quali-

---

[1]Muzafer Sherif, "Group Influences upon the Formation of Norms and Attitudes," in *Readings in Social Psychology*, eds. Eleanor E. Maccoby, Theodore M. Newcomb, and Eugene L. Hartley (New York: Holt, Rinehart & Winston, 1958), pp. 219–32.

[2]Muzafer Sherif, "Experiments on Norm Formation," in *Classic Contributions to Social Psychology*, eds. Edwin P. Hollander and Raymond G. Hunt (New York: Oxford University Press, 1972), pp. 320–29.

[3]Sherif, "Group Influences," p. 222.

fication, since rarely in daily living are we as isolated from external reference points as his subjects were in the autokinetic experiment. In fact, our constant contact with others gives us information that validates or challenges our subjective experience.

The second part of Sherif's experiment introduced social factors into the judgment of light movement. He formed groups of two and three people and asked each person to announce aloud his or her judgment of the distance the light point moved. Half the subjects judged the light movement alone first and then judged it in the presence of others. The other half judged it first in the presence of their group and then judged it alone.

To what extent did the individual decisions converge in the group situation? The greatest convergence occurred when people judged the light movement first in the presence of others. From his data, Sherif concluded that they continued to use the frame of reference developed in the presence of others. Also, the convergence of judgments in the reverse condition—that is, judgments alone first—was consistent and strong. When placed in groups, members of each group in the experiment arrived at a common frame of reference.

Why norms arise. A helpful way of viewing this experiment is provided by Leon Festinger in an analysis of the pressures or forces toward uniformity in groups.[4] Festinger's ideas may help us understand why group norms in the autokinetic experiment were so readily and consistently established.

Festinger says, "Opinions, attitudes, and beliefs which people hold must have some basis upon which they rest for their validity."[5] He proposes that validating or giving confidence to one's experience is quite different for tangible objects than for intangible attitudes and opinions. Visual or tactile perceptions are usually sufficient to verify or change one's attitude toward physical objects. If one measures the length of a board with a ruler, another's opinion about the length of the board will tend to make little difference in one's perception. Others' views, on the other hand, play an increasingly important role as opinions and beliefs are more abstract and less subject to evaluation by tactile, visual, or other direct experience.

Festinger identified a second type of pressure toward uniformity in groups. Often, progress toward a group goal requires some guides, standards, or uniformity for member behavior. Most groups need to have some minimum level of "togetherness" in order to do a task, and such "together-

[4]Leon Festinger, "Informal Social Communication," *Psychological Review*, 57 (1950), 271–82.

[5]Festinger, "Informal Social Communication," p. 272.

ness" implies common expectations for members' actions. Festinger states that pressures for uniformity will increase as (1) members feel that progress toward a goal would be aided by more uniform behavior, and (2) the achievement of individual goals becomes more dependent on the achievement of group goals.

Watching a light point in a totally darkened room approximates a simulation of perception in the "social reality" area. The absence of a physical frame of reference or of any direct experience with a moving light makes the judgments of distance more sensitive to the opinions of others. Information from others began to form external reference points for subjects in the Sherif autokinetic groups. Another's judgments provided at least *some* information in an ambiguous situation.

As many of the subjects may have realized, there was no inherent validity to the group's frame of reference. The group had no more valid way to establish a peculiar range and median for judging light movement than did individuals. Social norms, like judgments of autokinetic movement, are no more "real" than subjective reference systems. They do, though, provide a way of interpreting experience in an ambiguous situation. The views of others afford information, however incomplete, with which to compare one's subjective perceptions.

In organizations, people have expectations for others' actions, they have attitudes about appropriate conduct, and they have interpretations of events that occur. Each individual has a personal or subjective response and opinion to these situations, and yet they are, as social phenomena, inherently ambiguous and subject to processes of social validation. These elements give rise to the possibility of discord between one's subjective experience and apparent "social reality." We now proceed to examine the questions of what happens when one's subjective experience conflicts with perceptions of social norms, and what the consequences are of this conflict in organizational settings.

Subjective Versus Social Realities

Deviancy and self-doubt. Sherif carried his experiment one step further and opened a line of inquiry that is central to the focus of this chapter. It was, perhaps, an inevitable question arising from the autokinetic experiments described above: "Can we experimentally make the subject adopt a prescribed range and norm directed by specific social influences?"[6] How responsive and pliable, or how resistant and independent, is subjective experience in the face of a conflicting social reality?

[6]Sherif, "Group Influences," p. 229.

In an experiment developed from this question, Sherif placed one of his assistants in the autokinetic experiment with one of the assistant's close friends. The assistant had agreed with Sherif beforehand to attempt to "predetermine" the friend's judgments. The accomplice/assistant allowed her friend to judge the first several light movements alone. When the friend's reference point stabilized at about five inches, the assistant began to announce her own judgments at twelve inches. After several trials, they were both making judgments at twelve inches. The assistant then changed her judgments to three inches, and the friend gradually moved to this standard.

Sherif then suggested that the assistant make no more judgments, and he subsequently stated that the friend was underestimating the movement of the light. Her frame of reference changed again, to a longer judgment on each trial. It was soon after this that the friend whispered to the assistant, "Get me out of here!"[7]

Most readers can probably sympathize with her feelings; she appears to have been put through an Alice's Wonderland of the social psychologist's imagination. Was the experimenter asking the subject to question friendship and academic integrity in order to preserve a sense of rationality in the experiment? This result makes a point about the strength of external social reality, but probably in a context beyond the realm of daily experience.

Soloman Asch studied the effect of social pressure on individual opinion.[8] He placed subjects in a situation where the perceptual judgments of the rest of the group were in agreement with each other and at variance with the judgments of the subject.

The Asch experiment placed seven or eight people in chairs in a classroom and asked them to view two cards held by the experimenter. One card had three parallel lines of unequal length. The other card had a single line, similar in length to one of the lines on the first card. Participants were to announce which of the three lines on the first card matched the single line on the second card. All but one member of each group were in collusion with the experimenter to announce the same incorrect choice, and seating was prearranged so that the unsuspecting subject would be the last to announce a decision. The lines were drawn so that the correct choice was quite obvious—people judging them under ordinary conditions erred less than 1 percent of the time.

The experiment confronted people with weighing the influence of their subjective judgments against the influence of different judgments of others. The choice was whether to state a perception publicly that differed from the preannounced positions of the others, or whether to announce

[7]Sherif, "Group Influences," p. 230.

[8]Soloman E. Asch, *Social Psychology* (Englewood Cliffs, N.J.: Prentice-Hall, 1952), pp. 450–501.

a decision in line with the judgments of others. The situation created a dilemma in which subjects wanted both to be true to their own perceptions and to be consistent with the group. On the one hand, they stood to sacrifice their own opinions, and on the other hand, they risked feeling visible, different, and strange. Subjects in the experiment faced this choice point seven times out of a series of twelve different trials.

Largely from interviews with the subjects after the experiment, Asch learned something of the general experience they had had. First, the tension or pressure of conflicting forces existed for everyone; no one saw the other people's judgments as unimportant. Although attempts to explain away the discordant perceptions were made—instructions were misunderstood, different seating positions lead to different perceptions, and so forth—the subjects generally focused on themselves as the source of the difficulty and assumed the "burden of proof" for reconciling the difference.[9] In fact, Asch reveals that even though he, as experimenter, intellectually understood the structure of the situation, an impulse still existed to view the subject as the source of the problem. He says, "It is noteworthy that the experimenter, too, despite full knowledge of the situation at times perceives things in the same way, with the subject as the creator and center of disturbance."[10]

The post-experiment interviews indicated a widespread presence of self-doubt arising from the experiences of the subjects. Confusion, puzzlement, and doubt were present regardless of whether they had held to personal judgments or yielded to the group. There seemed to be a longing to be in agreement with the others, and they felt isolated in maintaining public differences. One person, who held strongly to personal perceptions, said, "Despite everything there was a lurking fear that in some way I did not understand I might be wrong; fear of exposing myself as inferior in some way. It is more pleasant if one is really in agreement."[11]

For several different research reports, Asch states that the number of judgments by subjects that conformed to the incorrect majority ranged from 33.2 to 36.8 percent.[12] Is this surprisingly low or distressingly high? For most people, these figures appear to be higher than expected, but here is certainly a situation where no definitive external frame of reference exists by which to appraise these percentages. The fact that some people chose to maintain their positions and others yielded to the group position simply suggests that the dilemma created for the participants was not simple—different people made different choices.

What conclusion can be drawn from the experiment? First, the

[9]Asch, *Social Psychology*, pp. 460–65.
[10]Asch, *Social Psychology*, p. 462.
[11]Asch, *Social Psychology*, p. 465.
[12]Asch, *Social Psychology*, p. 457; and Soloman E. Asch, "Opinions and Social Pressure," *Scientific American*, 193, 5 (1955), 3.

experiment illustrates the tension and anxiety resulting from the opposition of one's personal experience to the perceived experience of others. Second, the tendency for the participants and, at times, the experimenter to view the deviant as "the problem" was identified. But perhaps most relevant for the issues of this chapter, the experimenter observed a general rise of self-doubt in the subjects when they were confronted with a discrepancy between their personal experiences and the apparent experiences of others. The general desire was to be in group agreement, to not be visibly different, to be "at one with the group."

It appears that the important observation is about the *general* desire to be in agreement with an immediate social environment, and that feelings of self-confidence and esteem are frequently associated with the degree of felt unity or agreement. People take the threat or actual loss of this agreement quite seriously, even to the extent of yielding their independence of judgment, and in that sense some of their autonomy, for the social validation of opinions. Various forms of this process appear to be involved in organizational processes of socialization, indoctrination, and, in the extreme, brainwashing. Parallels of social pressure as an instrument of influence are common to POW camps, religious orders, and management development.[13]

Extensions of the experiment. Two additional points from the Asch experiments are worthy of mention. First, the degree to which tension exists in choosing between one's own and others' reported perceptual experiences is, up to a point, a function of the number of others present.[14] The presence of a single other person had negligible influence on the subjects, as indicated by practically all independent choices; the presence of two others seemed to increase the pressure substantially, as subjects yielded on almost 14 percent of the decisions; and the presence of three others raised the pressure again, as nearly 32 percent of the decisions across all subjects conformed to the majority view.

Also, the presence, in a group of seven or eight people, of an additional person who stated the *correct* answer reduced the pressure on subjects. When one "supporting partner" was present, incorrect answers were reduced to one-fourth of their earlier level.[15] These and other additional results suggest that the dilemma of choice between subjective and external references is strongly sensitive to the size and unanimity of "social reality." Given a break in that reality, in the form of only one

[13]Edgar H. Schein, "Management Development as a Process of Influence," *Industrial Management Review*, 2, 2, (1961).

[14]Asch, "Opinions and Social Pressure," p. 34.

[15]Asch, "Opinions and Social Pressure," p. 34.

opposing person or in the form of a supporting partner in the larger group, the problem of choice is reduced drastically.

A second extension of Asch's original study is also of interest. Using the same process of creating the experience of disagreement with a unanimous group for a naive individual, Crutchfield undertook additional studies of this type.[16] One of these studies concerned the influence of social pressure on contemporary social attitudes and opinions. Crutchfield gives this example: Subjects were asked to show agreement or disagreement with a number of statements while in a group of five people. One statement was, "Free speech being a privilege rather than a right, it is proper for a society to suspend free speech whenever it feels threatened." Only 19 percent of control subjects agreed with the statement, but 58 percent of the experimental subjects, facing a united front of four others, agreed.[17] Again, when asked, "Which of the following do you feel is the most important problem facing our country today?" and given five potential problems, such as economic recession, 48 percent of the experimental subjects chose "subversive activities" when apparently faced with a group consensus on this item. Only 12 percent of a control group chose this item.[18]

These attitudinal items, like the autokinetic effect, are highly subject to social influence. There is little opportunity, other than in interpersonal referents, to evaluate one's own impressions. Are they anomalies created by the unnatural and artificial laboratory situation, or do they have implications for decisions in organizations? We now turn to analyses of organizational decision making in order to evaluate the presence or absence of these principles in the "real" world and to attempt an assessment of their significance in the daily lives of people.

Social Pressures in a Jury Deliberation

One context in which the individual/group relationship may be salient is the process of jury decision. In this situation, the goal of the group is unanimity, which allows no room for differences. The only other option to the group is to report an inability to decide, and this may easily come to be equated with failure. One might reason that intense pressures for agreement may arise in this setting, and the dilemma of group versus self might be heightened. The popular movie, *Twelve Angry Men*, is a

[16]Richard S. Crutchfield, "Conformity and Character," *American Psychologist*, 10, 5 (1955), 191–98.
[17]Crutchfield, "Conformity and Character," p. 197.
[18]Crutchfield, "Conformity and Character," p. 197.

portrayal of the social pressures from and on a group majority in a jury decision. Along the same lines, the following is a personal account of one person, which illustrates, from his perspective and experience, the dilemma of individual and group in a jury:

> *Background.* The situation involves a trial by jury which was of wide interest and was closely followed by the press. The jury members were sequestered and were quite literally shut off from the world; our families, everyone. We were given a wing of rooms on an upper floor of a hotel. Each of us had our own room. We saw no TV, read only edited papers, our occasional telephone conversation with our families was monitored by either the bailiff or one of two court-appointed officials—we were isolated and insulated from the world in the most literal sense. Similarly, we were not permitted to discuss the trial in any manner with other jurors. Absolutely no comments or views were interchanged among the jury members. The consequent effect was the development of rather strong ties between the jury members; we became very friendly with one another. We felt we were "something special." We knew we were the focus of considerable attention, although we did not want to admit it at the time.
>
> Also, the twelve people on the jury were surprisingly compatible. We adapted to each other quickly and became friendly. Our goal was clearly defined, we had the attention of our peers, and, since we could not discuss the testimony, there was no conflict relative to achieving our common goal of a unanimous verdict. As a consequence, our morale was quite high and we genuinely felt that we were a team. We were indeed a solid group in the morning on which we heard our options as given by the judge.
>
> *Deliberations.* Our foreman, who was elected informally by consensus even before we were charged to do so, had a prestigious occupation and had clearly become the group's informal leader. The group consisted of seven men and five women; five persons with college degrees and seven without.
>
> After we were seated in the jury room, Bob, the foreman, began by discussing the case's high points objectively (I thought) and our options as to the verdict. Then he asked each of us, in turn, to review what we saw as the most important points in the testimony. Each of us followed this procedure and, with only minor exceptions, the discussions seemed straightforward with little apparent digression in the interpretation of the "facts." At this point we were reviewing testimony and making general statements with little bias as *overtly* perceived by the group members; there was virtually no display of emotion and I am sure that we were all confident of an early verdict; we seemed to be in accord. That is, there seemed to be agreement on the "facts" of the case, and these were discussed very

unemotionally. After everyone had a chance to discuss and respond, Bob suggested a vote by ballot. To my amazement, the result was seven for acquittal and five for conviction. It seemed to come as a shock to everyone on the jury when we failed to reach a consensus on the first ballot. The solidarity of the group had been dealt its first blow.

Bob again briefly reviewed the high points of the testimony and suggested that each of us again comment and give the rationale for voting as we did. While he was careful not to show his frustration, one could sense the tension. Indeed, the entire group evidenced this feeling to some degree. By the time we had completed the second review, from our own view we were no longer a team but two groups; we knew where each other stood in relation to the verdict. Everyone was certain originally, I am sure, we would reach an accord early, and now it appeared that we were very divergent in our views. It was quite a blow. At this point we (the majority) began to "talk" to the minority, trying to convince them of the error in their perceptions, quoting "facts." In short, we were "reasoning" with them. They quoted "facts" back. Bob, although he tried to remain neutral, made several pointed remarks which left no doubt about *his* position (acquittal). We took another secret ballot just before lunch. At that point it was nine for and three against.

Lunch, which was held in the jury room, was subdued, not at all like our previous lunches together. I recall we seemed to gravitate in small clusters, talking about the evidence. Since we all had agreed not to pressure or coerce any other jurors, we (the majority) talked amongst ourselves; the three against acquittal talked together—alone. During the course of the afternoon, tempers began to flare as the minority opinion holders remained intractable in the face of cold, hard facts. Frustration among both groups increased. By this time, the majority group began to consider the possibility that the jury might be hung (the standard for success would not be achieved). However, since there was a clear majority, we would not change our beliefs and vote differently. More pressure was placed upon the deviants. The tension grew as the conflict surfaced, and open "warfare" raged. The pressures to conform caused one additional person to "see the facts" before we adjourned for dinner, and the score stood at 10–2.

The feeling of hostility had been thick in the air as those who had previously held the minority opinion now were discussing the "facts" to support the majority opinion—they had "seen the light." The foreman, while still our leader, had long since joined in the discussion, giving us his personal views. We went to dinner at 6:30 feeling a tremendous amount of pressure and frustration. The dinner hour was characterized by a phenomenon as close to psychological amputation as I can imagine. I don't recall anyone speaking. While everyone was quiet that evening, I am sure the two deviants felt the quietness was *directed* at them.

Decision. After we returned, about 7:30, we immediately took another ballot (this had been suggested previously by the foreman). The score was now 11–1. The single holdout, Frank, was a person who could not verbalize his thoughts well and he never really was able to give us a good reason for his posture on the evidence. He became quite agitated during the afternoon and, after he became the sole "holdout," he literally screamed at the rest of us. He kept repeating, "he's guilty—I know he is!" We all, of course, tried to reason with him, but to no avail. About 9:30, Bob suggested we take a break and vote once more at 10:00. If nothing was resolved by then, he would ask the bailiff to excuse us for the night. I recall Frank was left all alone during this time; he didn't want to talk to anyone—nor did anyone apparently want to talk to him. Several jury members began playing cards; most just wanted to be alone with their thoughts. It was very quiet.

Finally, about 9:45 or so, Frank shouted, "All right—he's innocent!" I cannot describe the feeling of relief that pervaded that jury room. Bob asked, "Are you sure, Frank?" "Yes," said Frank. We all signed the verdict and sent it to the judge.[19]

It may be that the majority and minority people each faced a dilemma: The minority appeared to experience a conflict between their subjective judgments and social pressure from the rest of the jurors. The majority could very well have felt a tension between an aversion to pressing the minority, based on a commitment to each person's independence, and a desire for "right" to prevail and for the group to be successful. In many respects, the final structure of one versus eleven on this jury is similar to Asch's experiments, except that the majority were not confederates of the experimenter and had their own anxieties, ambivalences, and choices to live with. This example also highlights three of the stages of social pressure Leavitt perceives groups placing on deviant individuals: rationality, attack, and then isolation.[20]

The resolution of individual dilemmas in this jury was a process not without significance to external events and to people's lives. Someone—namely, the trial's defendant—was to be directly and strongly influenced by the social process and decision of the jury, and others may be indirectly influenced through the precedent of the decision. This is to affirm that the issue is not just of intellectual curiosity, but that it has real and significant consequences for others.

[19]Personal communication, Arthur Wycoff, Cleveland, Ohio.

[20]Harold J. Leavitt, *Managerial Psychology* (Chicago: University of Chicago Press, 1972), pp. 224–25.

Social Process, Self-esteem, and Institutional Policy

The Janis studies. An analysis of government policy making from the standpoint of group process has been conducted by Irving L. Janis of Yale University.[21] Janis initially became interested in the policy and operational decisions taken by President Kennedy and his advisors in the Bay of Pigs fiasco. He then embarked upon an inquiry to document the nature of the social or interpersonal process in several well-known government policy decisions. Janis analyzed in some detail four situations of policy failures: the Bay of Pigs, the U.S. invasion of North Korea, unpreparedness at Pearl Harbor in 1941, and the escalation of the Vietnam War by the introduction of bombing during the Johnson administration. As a counterpoint to these policy failures, he analyzed two policy successes, the Cuban missile crisis and the formulation of the Marshall Plan. His purpose was to cull out of these historical situations the nature of effective and ineffective group decision processes. This work provides a relevant assessment of whether group processes described above have meaningful implications for organizational and institutional behavior.

Janis's objective was ambitious, since the public records of internal policy deliberations are generally scant and usually not addressed to the questions most critical to his study. This is one of the hazards of doing research on questions of social import. One question is whether his analysis was not influenced by knowing the outcome of the event. For example, since he knew the Bay of Pigs invasion was a failure, would he tend to look for the negative factors of decision making in the historical records, and since he knew the Cuban missile crisis was successful, would he be predisposed to a favorable review of the events leading up to it? Although it was exploratory, Janis's work offers an unusual reconstructed picture of the policy process in terms of the issues of this chapter. The present approach will be to draw from his research where the analysis is most convincing and the issues are most relevant to the issues under analysis here.

Primarily through his investigations of the four policy "failures" mentioned above, Janis identifies eight symptoms of ineffective decision making. Summarizing, these are:

1. An illusion of invulnerability
2. Rationalizations that discount warnings contrary to the group's assumptions
3. Ignoring the ethical or moral consequences of decisions

[21]Irving L. Janis, *Victims of Groupthink* (Boston: Houghton Mifflin, 1972).

4. Stereotyped views of the outgroup or enemy

5. Social pressure toward dissenters

6. Self-censorship, leading to minimization of doubts and counterarguments

7. A shared illusion of unanimity

8. The emergence of members to protect the group from adverse information about the effectiveness or morality of its decisions[22]

Of these characteristics, which together are labeled "groupthink" by Janis, one aspect stands out in relevance to the present discussion. This is self-censorship, or the degree to which people either suppress, withhold, or modify their true feelings and beliefs in policy meetings. This process appears to correspond to that in the Asch experiment, where there was a general increase in self-doubt by a subject in an apparent minority position. In a policy group, a shared illusion of unanimity seems to be a direct consequence of this self-censorship effect. Also, putting social pressure on dissenters can be viewed simply as applying to others the same censorship applied to oneself.

The clearest statement of this process in Janis's studies is the reported reflections of Arthur Schlesinger and others of the events and meetings leading up to the Bay of Pigs fiasco. Schlesinger was one of about a dozen advisors in policy and planning meetings that included top officials in the State, Defense, and Treasury departments, the Attorney General, White House staff advisors, the Joint Chiefs of Staff, and CIA officials. Janis reviews Schlesinger's description of how he withheld his doubts and criticisms of the invasion plan in policy meetings. The fact that Schlesinger had strong reservations about the invasion proposal is evident from his private communications with Kennedy; yet he failed to present his views when issues were being discussed and policy was formulated in the group. He stated that his feeling at the time was that he would have been unlikely to influence the group away from the invasion plan and would probably have succeeded only in giving himself "a name as a nuisance."[23]

It appears that Schlesinger was not alone in the role of "silent dissenter." From various sources it was reported that Secretary of State Rusk asked more penetrating and critical questions of his associates than he did in the policy meetings, that Secretary of Defense McNamara held assumptions about the invasion that were at variance from its general concept, and that the Joint Chiefs had serious doubts about the plan from a military standpoint. Indeed, there appeared to be more than a few unexpressed questions and reservations about the invasion plan. On

[22]Janis, *Victims*, pp. 197–98.
[23]Janis, *Victims*, p. 40.

the basis of discussions with the meeting participants after the ill-fated invasion, Theodore Sorenson concluded, "Doubts were entertained but never pressed, partly out of a fear of being labelled 'soft' or undaring in the eyes of their colleagues."[24] It appears that the risk of seeming strange or weak, or of receiving social disapproval, was an inhibiting force on the full participation of those involved.

The main psychological function of "groupthink" is to maintain the self-esteem of members in cohesive groups. To the extent that a group seeks concurrence rather than critical analysis and appraisal, the group is serving to protect the individual members from feelings of personal inadequacy, it is providing a sense of security, and it is avoiding the emotional strain of disagreement. Janis states that group members naturally cope with the stress of decision making by striving for mutual support.

In discussing the psychological function of self-censorship for individuals in a policy group, he states:

> One of the norms that is likely to become dominant during a crisis involves living up to a mutual nonaggression pact. Each individual in the group feels himself to be under an injunction to avoid making penetrating criticisms that might bring on a clash with fellow members and destroy the unity of the group. Adhering to this norm promotes a sense of collective strength and also eliminates the threat of damage to each participant's self-esteem from hearing his own judgments on vital issues criticized by respected associates.[25]

The implication of Janis's work is that in "real life" as well as in the small group laboratory, it is "more pleasant to be in agreement." There appears, to some extent, to be an innate trade-off between group-provided esteem and one's complete independence of thought. To maintain one's critical analysis may mean to sacrifice group equanimity or even one's group membership, and to risk one's degree of social esteem. On the other hand, to choose for emotional support may be at a cost to one's independence of judgment. At least, Janis's analysis of the Bay of Pigs deliberations, and possibly other public decisions as well, indicate that these trade-offs do occur in institutional settings and that they do have significant consequences for the numerous people not directly involved in the policy foundation. In this sense, the dilemma of social esteem versus independence has ramifications far beyond the immediate actors.

The Bay of Pigs analysis illustrates the problem of individuals' choosing group harmony at the expense of their better judgments. What is the

---

[24]Janis, *Victims*, p. 40.
[25]Janis, *Victims*, p. 205.

experience of membership in a group that is choosing critical judgment at the expense of group equanimity? As mentioned earlier, Janis provides two examples of the antithesis of "groupthink"—the Cuban missile crisis and the development of the Marshall Plan. These case descriptions suggest an answer to this question. Various phrases, some taken directly from the statements of participants and some Janis's own characterization of their feelings on the basis of his research, convey the experience of the participants in these policy-forming groups: "painful emotion," "impatience," "subjective discomfort," "sleeplessness," "protracted turmoil," "unpleasant bickering," "agitated feelings," "subjective distress," "acute distress," "agony of critical appraisal," "remarkably painful group experience," "intellectual agony," "endless debates."[26] In general, the stress of a crisis-oriented group and the uncertainties created by looking deeply and honestly at the issues created emotional turmoil for the group participants. To remain as completely independent in thinking and expression as possible meant being critical and even destructive of another's ideas. Also, an unswervingly critical attitude toward the ideas of others risked the others' resentment and rejection.

In his discussion of the missile crisis, Janis mentions both the strong need of the members for emotional support and the inability of the group to provide it:

> Knowing that one misstep could precipitate a devastating nuclear war, the members' need for emotional support from the group was undoubtedly very high, but most of the time the lack of consensus frustrated this need, depriving the members of a sense of unity that would have enabled them to feel more confident about a successful outcome.[27]

The encouragement of difference and dissent is also a confrontation with the fact that the group may, in fact, be unsuccessful. In the Cuban missile crisis, Janis states, the participants experienced the "acute distress of being reminded that their collective judgments could be wrong."[28] To move away from a belief of invulnerability, away from a false sense of group security, and away from a distortion of the situation is to look directly at one's own and the group's insecurity. Stereotypes about one's own group's strength and morality and about other groups' undesirability are convenient ways of avoiding one's lack of certainty. To maintain a high level of honesty in a group about the group may be to experience a disturbing collective insecurity.

[26]Janis, *Victims*, pp. 138–81.
[27]Janis, *Victims*, p. 154.
[28]Janis, *Victims*, p. 165.

The recollections of Albert Speer. Albert Speer, minister of Armaments and war production of the Third Reich from 1942 to 1945, wrote of his experience as a leader in the German war effort of World War II. In *Inside the Third Reich,* Speer's reflections on his own actions and feelings vis-à-vis his independence of judgment and the centrality of his position are poignant illustrations of this dilemma of choice.[29] Of course, Speer's recollections of his involvement in events may be faulty, or he may be failing to state his knowledge exactly in his memoirs. However, for the present purposes, let us take his statements at face value.

Through a series of chance events in his career as a young architect in the 1930s, Speer was catapulted to an influential position as Hitler's chief architect. This was a position of intimacy with Hitler, since Hitler fancied himself as an artist/architect and assumed intense personal leadership, interest, and involvement in the building plans and designs for the Third Reich. As a man of only 28, inexperienced but ambitious, Speer found himself in an incredibly close relationship with the Fuehrer and in a most remarkably influential role in architectural developments in Nazi Germany. This relationship later proved to be the basis for a central managerial position in the German war effort.

Speer's memoirs illustrate the interrelationships between the centrality of his position among Hitler's ministers, Speer's level of self-esteem, and his degree of independence of thought and action in relation to Hitler. In January 1944, Speer was hospitalized, owing to his physical deterioration from an accident and from the mental stress of his increasing personal setbacks, resentments, and disappointments in the political intrigues among Hitler's top advisors. The political maneuvers, led principally by Bormann, Himmler, and Goering, intensified during the five months that Speer was away from active work. In this period, he felt he was receiving less respect and honor from Hitler than he had previously received and currently deserved, and he suffered a decrease in his organizational power as a result of the encroaching influence of his political foes. Speer experienced these blows most severely in the early period of his illness, and their impact on him was not only depression and disappointment but also the slow emergence of a new perspective on Hitler and the course Speer had been pursuing at his side. His decline in centrality and associated loss of esteem and emotional strength gradually led Speer to a position of greater independence from Hitler and his policies. The first signs of this change, he recalls, took place several months after his hospitalization:

> My injured self-esteem, the sense of having been personally offended, was certainly operative ... when I wrote him a letter frankly questioning these decisions. This was the first of a long series of letters

[29]Albert Speer, *Inside the Third Reich,* trans. Richard and Clara Winston (New York: Avon Books, 1971).

and memoranda in which, frequently concealed behind disagreements on matters of fact, I began to show some independence.[30]

Angry and discouraged at his diminished role, Speer was soon on the verge of resigning his position, or at least withdrawing to the point of effective resignation. At this point, strong support was mobilized for him among the country's industrialists and among influential people in the government. Their arguments persuaded Speer not to resign, and he eventually regained his former power base and his centrality to Hitler. Speer recalls his thinking at the point at which he knew his political battles had been won and he had regained a favored position with the Fuehrer:

> Up to 1942, I still felt that my vocation as an architect allowed me a measure of pride that was independent of Hitler. But since then I had been bribed and intoxicated by the desire to wield pure power, to assign people to this and that, to say the final word on important questions, to deal with expenditures in the billions. I thought I was prepared to resign, but I would have sorely missed the heady stimulus that comes with leadership. . . . To be sure, our relationship had developed a crack; my loyalty had become shaky, and I sensed that it would never again be what it had been. But for the present I was back in Hitler's circle—and content.[31]

From Speer's descriptions, the relationship was never the same again, and he not only came to argue strongly against many of Hitler's policies toward the end of the war, and even to disobey or counteract some decisions, but at one point he undertook the exploration of a plan to assassinate Hitler.

These fragments of Speer's reflections on his feelings and behavior as armaments minister points to a relationship between his power, his centrality, and the maintenance of his self-esteem. As indicated earlier in this chapter, esteem, and in that sense a security of self, can easily and frequently be tied to the satisfaction of a particular role in a social group. This security seemed to restrict independence of thought and action for Speer, since his feelings and actions became more independent as his social importance and self-security declined.

Roles for Integrating Membership and Independence

As with many of these dilemmas, it is easy to overdraw the distinction and to present the dilemma as solely either/or. At points of conflict between group norms and individual preferences, the choice of a group member

[30]Speer, *Inside the Third Reich*, p. 433.
[31]Speer, *Inside the Third Reich*, pp. 439–40.

is rarely as stark as capitulation to the group or ejection from it. If a situation were extreme in the choices it offered, a decision might be easier to make than if conflicting criteria of choice are each only moderately strong. The lack of apparent extreme consequences contributes to the nature of the dilemma.

The choice in groups is rarely between capitulation and exclusion, since groups do adjust to the influence of specific individuals. Certainly, one dimension of membership can be to attempt to change group norms. Also, self-esteem is increased not only through acceptance and confirmation by others; one's self-respect may also be enhanced as one acts in terms of personal preference and beliefs, regardless of the views of others.

Ibsen's Dr. Stockmann.   These points are particularly well illustrated through the figure of Dr. Stockmann in Ibsen's play, *A Public Enemy*.[32] Dr. Stockmann is a physician strongly committed to the highest principles of conduct in his Norwegian community, in his family, and in himself. Through scientific testing, he discovers a health threat to users of the town's popular natural baths, which attract many people to the community and are a considerable economic asset to the town. His discovery puts the short-run profitability of the baths into question and places him in severe conflict with community leaders, who respond to their own immediate economic interests. In addition, the "solid majority" of the community allows itself to be influenced and controlled by the so-called liberal community leaders in the maintenance of self-serving and expedient social myths.

As Dr. Stockmann almost naively pursues his exposure of this problem, he increasingly finds a withdrawal of the local people from their stated values and a retreat to self-interests. Dr. Stockmann is threatened with loss of personal and family security, as pressure grows to have him retract his independent views. Stockmann's choice is to refuse to yield to these pressures. In fact, in making this decision, he gains optimism, energy, and self-confidence in affirming his ideals through his actions. After being isolated from community support, rejected by his wife's foster father as a benefactor, and disclaimed by teachers, landlord, and most friends, Dr. Stockmann gains confidence and strength from his independent position. His ability to act according to his conscience, regardless of the external social response, indicates that he has found a different and internal reference point for his self-esteem. "Why, I'm the strongest man in the place," he declares.[33] Stockmann is now defining his strength in terms of his own sense of right and values, rather than

[32]Henrik Ibsen, *A Public Enemy*, trans. Peter Watts (Baltimore: Penguin 1964).
[33]Ibsen, *A Public Enemy*, p. 218.

in the more conventional terms of socially defined status, influence, and material security. He has clearly passed any point of ambivalence toward the worldly costs of this position, which allows him to feel undaunted, invincible, and, once again, certain of himself and his role in the society.

Dr. Stockmann's immediate impulse after his exclusion from his community is to withdraw—to leave Norway and go to America. However, his second response, and the position that gives him his greatest strength and courage, is to fight for social reform. He decides to stay and work within his community, seeking to realize his ideals in the community he loves: He will open his own school, and his first enrollments will be aimless street boys. Would he be successful? What chances would this endeavor have of ever changing the norms and values of his community? These questions are less important than the fact that he does see and take whatever opportunity is available to him to bring his community's practices closer to his ideals.

Dr. Stockmann's action illustrates a choice to remain part of his community or group and to work within it for change. Even though his role is one of deviant, he feels reform can be achieved from within, and he commits himself to this pursuit.

George Ball in the Vietnam debate.   Another example of a dissenter who was firm, independent, and confident in his minority role appears to have been George Ball, undersecretary of state during the initiation and the escalation of bombing of North Vietnam. By the account of David Halberstam in *The Best and the Brightest*, George Ball held a strongly dissenting view of the policy to bomb North Vietnam, beginning in 1964, throughout 1965, and through most of 1966.[34] Janis used this policy decision as an example of groupthink and briefly discussed Ball as a "domesticated dissenter," a person whose opposing opinion is not seriously considered and whose opposition is controlled by group sanctions. However, Halberstam's analysis is a more detailed assessment of Ball's role and motivations, identifying an alternative strategy for group membership that is neither capitulation to or expulsion from the group. Halberstam presents Ball as a man of independent thought, a man whose career in government was based on independence and ability: "He was a man of considerable zest, enthusiasm and egocentrism, and he did not defer to those around him in Washington."[35]

Over the year and a half of the painful process by which the administration came to the decision to initiate and then escalate the bombing

[34]David Halberstam, *The Best and the Brightest* (Greenwich, Conn.: Fawcett Publications, 1972).
[35]Halberstam, *The Best and the Brightest*, p. 598.

of North Vietnam, George Ball consistently and forcefully identified the weaknesses of the bombing policy, not in a "domesticated" and empty role, as suggested by Janis, but as a serious and strong input to the decision process. Halberstam evaluates Ball's role as substantially slowing down the process of decision because of the doubts he raised in the minds of others, particularly Lyndon Johnson. Ball was clearly working within the established framework of the policy group, utilizing memos, papers, and meetings to press his views. His behavior, as opposed to his views, was in all ways consistent with the general norms of the group, and there is no evidence of an interpersonal animosity or resentment between himself and the others. For the critical years, George Ball appears to have developed a role for which he suffered neither doubts about his self-worth nor social pressures for conformity. The other aspects of group-think may apply to this policy decision or to the other members of the group, but George Ball appears more to have maintained an effective integration of membership and dissent.

The two examples of Dr. Stockmann and George Ball offer models of people who come to terms with the dilemma of membership and independence in different ways. In neither case was the individual required to totally leave the group in order to maintain his independent thought. Each found a basis for a social role that was affirming to himself and that he found constructive. These examples serve as models capable of integrating personal needs and social roles.

CHAPTER REVIEW

The essence of social organization is the ability to provide continuity and stability to a collection of people engaged in purposive action. Concerted, collective action is dependent on establishment and maintenance of norms of behavior; norms are a behavioral adhesive that make social organization possible. No collective action would exist in the absence of commonly held expectations for behavior among group, organizational, or institutional members.

Inherent in the ability to provide continuity and stability is the limitation of choices and actions of individuals. Social stability does not, in other words, come without a price to individual members. This quality gives rise to a potential dilemma of choice between the individual's ideas and preferences and the actions expected of him or her by membership in the social organization. By its very nature, social organization cannot be all things to all people, and thus, the possibility arises that a person's judgments and ideas may be at variance with those of others in his or her immediate social environment.

As we have seen in the various materials in this chapter, several additional factors are often present. The person's sense of identity or self-esteem may be tied to one's association with others, and the exercise of independent action may be at the expense of this emotional support. It is also important to note that there are alternatives to the apparently disastrous consequences of "standing alone." If Dr. Stockmann's symbolic stance and George Ball's policy positions are representative of an aspect of human experience, esteem and peace of mind can be gained from an internal frame of reference. There is potential security on the side of maintaining one's independence, even though this may involve creating a stressful relationship with the social expectations of one's group.

The choices we face in our daily lives in relation to group and institutional membership may seem mundane in relation to the significance of some of the situations described in this chapter. And to most of us, the values to be gained may seem slight in relation to the personal costs to be paid for maintaining independence. Yet it is possible to be lulled into a weakened sense of awareness and thus to yield full responsibility for choice.

What are the implications of this dilemma in administrative behavior? One implication is that the manager's self-view is both dependent and independent of group membership. Most people receive emotional security and self-confirmation by being in consonance with others and with social expectations. Most people also gain self-worth and validation from their unique self-expression, regardless of its relation to social expectations. Managers are inevitably members of groups and subject to these opposing pulls of the self. The manager is both social member and autonomous person; the role of administrator calls for both promoting social harmony and exercising an individual conscience. The relation of person to group is a fundamental and inevitable problem in human associations and the basis for a dilemma in administrative behavior.

Chapter **6**

Leadership Requirements for Adhering to and Changing Group Norms
a leadership dilemma created by
stable organizations
and a changing society

Group norms were presented in the preceding chapter as an essential ingredient of social organization. This mechanism provides for continuity of member activities and efforts. Norms also represent expectations, guides, and constraints for individual behavior that may occasionally be counter to individual ideals and preferences. Group membership contains an inherent dilemma of choice for individuals as organizational members, and outcomes of the dilemma are a significant factor in organizational behavior.

This statement, however, represents only one side of the relationship of individuals and organizations. Just as organizations may require stability and individuals may seek independence from social expectations, it is equally true that organizations require flexibility and individuals seek continuity and stability. In other words, both individuals and organizations are adaptive systems: Both have forces toward maintenance and stability and toward growth and change. This chapter explores the nature and consequences of choice where the tension lies between the system's needs for flexibility and change and the individual's needs for stability and continuity.

The topic of organizational change and adaptation has received increasing popular and academic interest in the past decade. Perhaps the best-known popular work has been Alvin Toffler's *Future Shock*, with its portrayal of the need for flexible organizations, or "Ad-hocracies."[1] Re-

---

[1]Alvin Toffler, *Future Shock* (New York: Bantam, 1970).

lated to this perspective are John Gardner's prescription for self-renewing organizations,[2] and Warren Bennis's view that society is moving toward temporary organizational systems.[3] Whether in the form of predictions, prescriptions, or exhortations, the issue of social and organizational flexibility in a changing society has received wide interest.

The economic, technical, social, and political environments of organizations do appear to be engaged in a high rate of change. Changing economic conditions afford opportunities and create necessities for restructuring the resources and assets of a business or agency. Technical developments require greater organizational innovation and development. Social mores shift, necessitating changes in organizational norms. New societal influences, such as the consumer movement, force attention to formerly deemphasized values. All or most of these external changes are likely to exist concurrently for present-day organizations and to generate internal forces for change. Yet any change implies the unfamiliar, the unfamiliar implies risk, and risk implies choice.

Environmental change is pervasive and can result in requirements for organizational members to learn new skills, or to acquire new information or new attitudes and opinions. It also may affect the manner in which groups operate, by requiring new work procedures, revision of group values and traditions, or development of more effective group communication and decision making. Each of these aspects of groups is reflected in group norms, or the accustomed and expected ways of activity and interaction in groups. The focus of this chapter is on the tension between the continuity and stability provided by group norms and an organization's need for change that is instigated by a requirement for external adaptation.

A person in a leadership capacity carries a dual responsibility: that of ensuring both organizational flexibility and stability. A leader unquestionably has a strong influence on group and institutional norms and carries responsibility for adapting the organization to wider social, technical, and economic conditions. However, his own capacity to lead is constrained by the values and norms of the organization or group. A leader typically has some latitude in instigating or initiating normative change, and yet group norms are a powerful constraint on a leader's ability to initiate change. To introduce needed change may threaten a person's capacity to lead, but by not introducing needed change, the leader may default on institutional responsibilities.

This chapter begins with an analysis of the leader's dilemma of

[2]John W. Gardner, *Self Renewal: The Individual and the Innovative Society* (New York: Harper & Row, 1964).

[3]Warren G. Bennis, *Changing Organizations* (New York: McGraw-Hill, 1966).

adhering to and of changing group norms. In the theory of leadership, in laboratory studies of leader/group relationships, and in observations of leaders in actual groups, this dilemma is identified. Knowledge from each of these areas suggests that a leader's capacity to influence is dependent on an adherence to group norms. A leader may experience responsibilities deriving from an organizational role, yet his actions are guided, to some extent, by his relationship to group norms and values. Various writers have identified the conflict of these two expectations, a dilemma of leadership. In a recent example, a naval leader's attempts to revise traditional rules and codes of conduct are examined in terms of leader/group relations and the issues of organizational change and member stability. In another case, a major technical improvement in naval firing failed to be accepted because of the naval leadership's commitment to traditional means of operation.

A second aspect of group norms relates to the nature of communication between group members. Generally, norms are established wherein individuals are relatively certain of an idea before introducing it to the group, or are fairly likely to have the support of others before expressing their level of satisfaction in the group. One particular study illustrates that group decision making improves as members can be less cautious in expressing their ideas and feelings. The study also showed that this is easier to do privately than publicly. A leader's responsibility for effective group communication and decision making may lead to encouraging greater risk taking in group discussion, but the same person's needs for a stable group may lead him/her not to encourage this process. This dilemma of the leader in relation to the "openness" of group communication is another dimension of the problem of organizational change.

Adhering to and Changing Norms

A leadership paradox. Any organizational leader needs to gain and maintain the confidence of group members. In general, good relations are a source of mutual satisfaction, sought by both leaders and members; and given this need, one might expect group leaders to represent and closely adhere to group norms and values. This principle has been documented in a study of farming communities in Kentucky. This study discovered that farming neighborhoods that valued change in farming methods and adoption of government-recommended practices had leaders who were the most innovative farmers.[4] The leaders of communities whose

---

[4]C. Paul Marsh and A. Lee Coleman, "Farmers' Practice-Adoption Rates in Relation to Adoption Rates of 'Leaders,'" *Rural Sociology*, 19, No. 2 (1954), 180–81.

regard for change and improvement was relatively low were generally not more innovative than the rest of the farmers. The authors found support for their hypothesis that "if the residents of a neighborhood place a high value on innovations . . . , they will go to innovators for informa tion; but, on the other hand, if the residents are resistant to innovations, the 'leaders' whose advice is sought are unlikely to be innovators."[5] This study implies that either people seeking leadership conformed to group norms and values, or people were chosen as leaders who represented important community values; the point is that leadership status and conformance to group norms were associated. The leader of a group that values change will be an innovator. Leaders of groups with other dominant values will strongly manifest those particular values.

But the relationship of leaders and group norms is unlikely to be as simple as the view that group leaders are mere representatives of group values. The other side of leadership is to initiate group action and to introduce necessary change for the good of the group, even if such actions run counter to initial member desires. The leader cannot simply be the best follower, for one who does not initiate for the group is not a leader. Yet if a group is to have an ability for adaptation, one of the areas for leadership is group norms. A paradox of leadership is the problem of how group leaders can conform to group norms *and* act to change them at the same time.

Idiosyncrasy credit. Social psychologist Edwin Hollander has developed a theory of status and conformity that addresses this apparent contradiction.[6] He makes a distinction between compliance with specific group expectations for the leadership role and compliance with general group norms. The former is a matter of close conformity, the latter has more flexibility. The leaders of progressive farming communities discussed above, Hollander might argue, were "required" to adhere to the farmers' expectations for innovation. On the other hand, there might be other areas of general group norms, such as the type of car driven or typical recreational activities and interests, on which deviation would be tolerated. Hollander's answer to the paradox of leadership is that some areas of group expectations are specific to the leader and are more intolerant of deviation than others.

Hollander proposed another resolution of this paradox, which is the difference between gaining leadership and exercising it once it is attained. He suggests that status is gained and increased by a group member by conformity with group norms and by clear contributions to the group

5Marsh and Coleman, "Farmers," pp. 180–81.
6Edwin P. Hollander, "Conformity, Status, and Idiosyncrasy Credit," *Psychological Review*, 65, (1958), 117–27.

task. The status gained in the early period of group membership then serves as a "credit" to be used by a high-status individual in deviating from group norms—what Hollander calls idiosyncratic behavior. "Idiosyncrasy credit" gives latitude for deviance to a high-status person in a group. However, the deviance cannot be sustained indefinitely without risk to the person's status. If the group does not change or the leader does not reconform to the group norm, available idiosyncrasy credits will be depleted, and an exhausted supply implies pressures for exclusion from the group. Deviating from group norms will diminish credits at a rate that depends on the degree and relevancy of the nonconforming activity. Deviating from specific group expectations for leader behavior, as with a leader of an innovative farming community who is not progressive, diminishes credits rapidly.

Hollander's framework appears a plausible explanation of the leadership paradox described above, and it is consistent with a number of experimental studies of status and conformity in groups. Yet it lacks the specifics of leadership behavior in relating to groups and does not develop the choices faced by leaders in maintaining or attempting to alter group norms.

Changing institutionalized norms. How are conflicting requirements of introducing change reflected in actual choices and behaviors of leaders? A classic small group experiment by Ferenc Merei responds to this question.[7] Merei observed children in two-day nurseries, noting all interactions taking place between the children over a two-week period. On the basis of these observations, certain children were selected, formed into experimental groups, and given a separate room with familiar nursery toys, furniture, and tools. The children so selected were not leaders: All exhibited more "following orders" than "giving orders," imitated others more than they were imitated by others, and were average in their nurseries in terms of participation, cooperation, and aggression. The idea of the experiment was to allow the newly formed groups to play alone until "institutionalization," stability of habits and traditions, had been achieved.

Twelve groups, homogenous as to sex and similar in age, were created in this way. All groups had six or fewer children. Merei reported that "an assembly was considered a group when it developed a relatedness, with permanent rules, habits, traditions, entirely of its own." Such traditions consisted of seating location, possession of play objects, ceremonies associated with play, expressions of belonging together, rituals, sequence of games, group jargon, and so forth.

[7]Ferenc Merei, "Group Leadership and Institutionalization," in *Readings in Social Psychology*, eds. Eleanor E. Maccoby, Theodore M. Newcomb, and Eugene L. Hartley (New York: Holt, Rinehart & Winston, 1958), pp. 522–31.

After these patterns had developed, one new member, especially chosen for his or her exhibited initiative and direction in the general nursery, was introduced into each experimental group. The child added to each group was also older than the other members of the group, and was observed to rank high on being imitated, giving orders, and aggression toward others. Over the course of the experiment, each of 26 such "leaders" was placed at some time with one or another of the twelve groups. The study was designed to determine whether individual leaders or the traditions of the experimental groups were stronger. Would the older children establish leadership roles in their new groups, or would they be dominated by the customs of the group? Would the groups be changed by the new member, and if so, through what methods would change be introduced?

Merei's general conclusions were quite dramatic. Regardless of the previous relationship of the leader and the group members, and regardless of the fact that on a one-to-one basis the older child was more dominating than each group member, the leaders proved surprisingly weak against the group traditions. Merei stated:

> ... In a group possessing traditions, the leader introduced does not become the source of new habits and rules; rather, he will be the one to take over existing group traditions and thus to follow a model. This happens in spite of the fact that in the larger social formation [day nursery] he had served as a model to every member of the group.[8]

Behind this general conclusion lay some interesting and instructive differences in the way individual "leaders" approached group traditions. In most cases, the leader was forced to accept the group traditions but still managed to play the role of the leader. Merei identified three distinct styles for achieving conformity to the group *and* leadership of it. The first type of approach was termed the "order-giver." After an initial rebuff at directing, the child would quickly learn the norms and habits of the group and begin instructing group members to do exactly what they would have done anyway. This behavior appeared to be an acceptable accommodation between leader and members and created, as Merei comments, a situation in which the leader imitated the group and the members followed the orders of their imitator.

A second dominant approach was termed the "proprietor." In these cases, the new group "leader" took possession of all the toys and furniture in the room and put himself in charge of their use, again exactly according to the traditions previously established by the group. The new

[8]Merei, "Group Leadership," p. 525.

leader established control by "owning" the play materials and taking things away from other children, but was himself taken in by the group and strongly influenced in that the toys were still used in highly ritualized and patterned ways.

The third approach of leaders was both more subtle and more penetrating. After an initial attempt and failure to direct the group, the new leader would quickly learn and follow group traditions. Then, in the course of an activity, the leader would introduce slight, seemingly insignificant variations into the activity. For example, one leader joined in a traditional block game, but suggested that the red side of a block always be on top. The group tradition was not changed, but it was also not exactly the same. From this beginning, the leader gradually introduced new elements and greater variations of the games and traditions. This style, termed the "diplomat," required a high level of activity, exceptional social skill, and initiative by the child.

Merei suggests that this study illustrates the existence of a group reality that goes beyond the separate experiences of individual members: "It is tradition, the carrier of which is the individual, who, in turn, is strengthened by it." The study also shows that group leadership is not independent of this group reality, that the relation between leadership and group norms is one of mutual influence and accommodation. Where "natural" leaders were introduced into "institutionalized" groups, generally both leaders and groups were influenced. The extreme cases of complete assimilation of a "leader" or of complete altering of group traditions were exceedingly rare. Leaders were typically seen to adhere to the group norms while establishing some basis of leadership and domination, although some bases of influence had very little, if anything, to do with changing the actual play activities of the children. Only in the relatively infrequent cases of the "diplomat" were group traditions substantially modified. In most cases, there appeared to be domination with no normative, or tradition-related, innovation.

The results of the Merei experiment are instructive in terms of the change/stability issue of this chapter. First, the study illustrates the force toward stability carried through habits and group traditions. In nearly all cases, these traditions and their attendant stability were not trivial issues; they turned out to be stronger than an older, more aggressive child, familiar with the role of directing and organizing others' activities. Group norms, established within only three to six play periods of the experimental groups, were surprisingly resistant to change. We are led by Merei's report to infer that in most groups in this experiment, stability prevailed over adaptation. The requirements of imagination and skill for the "diplomat" were apparently not met by many of the 26 children placed in the groups as leaders.

Second, the older children introduced into the groups obtained a basis of influence and avoided being dominated by the groups. In terms of behavior, the older children might try to gain membership at the risk of being controlled by existing traditions, or they might try to maintain leader activities at the risk of isolation and exclusion from the group. Most leaders resolved this dilemma by accommodating themselves and finding a basis for leadership within the group's traditions.

Leadership in natural groups.   Applying Merei's experimental study of nursery-school groups to problems of organizational behavior involves a large, and perhaps questionable, extrapolation. The presence of a leadership dilemma is an inference from the study, not a conclusion of it. In addition, Merei's groups existed, as far as we know, in stable external environments. The leaders' roles in the groups might have been significantly altered if a widely perceived external threat to the group existed. Fortunately, the nature of leader/group relationships has not alone been the focus of studies in the experimental laboratory; turning to studies of natural groups brings the discussion more into the direct realm of organizational behavior.

Several of the most thorough studies of group behavior, analyzed in terms relevant to this chapter, are presented in George Homan's widely known book, *The Human Group*.[9] Homans's analysis of two studies, in particular, bears upon a leader's relationship to group norms. The first of these is the study of the bank-wiring room from the famous Hawthorne studies, which played a key role in the emergence of the human relations movement in industry. This was a study of a work group of men who wired and assembled telephone switchboard banks. A man named Taylor was the emerging informal leader of this work group. Taylor's activities and relationship to group members are of greatest interest in this chapter.

A second group reviewed and analyzed by Homans is the Norton Street gang. The original study of this group was done by W.F. Whyte and was reported in his book, *Street Corner Society*. A man named Doc, leader of the street gang, is of particular interest in the present context.

Homans's discussion of the bank-wiring group pays close attention to Taylor's standing with group members and to his behavior in relation to group norms. In terms of patterns of group interaction and the feelings of group members, Taylor was the most popular man among the workers. He also, as Homans reveals, most closely held to the ideals of behavior in the group. Specifically, Taylor was a skillful and dependable wireman, and his work output conformed to members' accepted idea of a proper day's work more closely than that of any other worker except one, who

[9]George Homans, *The Human Group* (New York: Harcourt Brace Jovanovich, 1950).

matched him in this regard. Taylor never produced below group expectations, he never "squealed" on a group member, and he was never con-
descending toward others. Of the two subgroups of workers, he was a
member of the higher-status group. Taylor was clearly the person most
consistently adhering to group norms. At the conclusion of the study, he
was emerging in the role of managing relationships external to the group
and initiating activities within the group. In short, Taylor was becoming
the dominant leader of the group.

Homans's analysis of Doc, leader of the Norton Street gang, similarly
concludes that the leader is the person best living up to the standards and
values of the group. Athletic activities were a central aspect of the gang's
interactions, and Doc was indeed skilled as a boxer and a bowler. Of
course, these were the valued athletics of the gang partly because Doc
was good at them, and he was good at them in the group partly because
he was the leader. The important point is that Doc was of highest social
rank in the group and the best consistent athletic performer. In other
areas as well, Doc conformed to group values: He responded to demands
of others for help more than did anyone else in the group; in quarrels
within the group, Doc heard the various sides and acted as judge, settling
the issue. In these cases, Doc was expected to best uphold the group's
sense of fairness and justice—to put aside his personal considerations,
where others were allowed to side with their friends. In these ways, Doc
was seen to best embody the norms of the group.

Homans states that to rank high in a group, one must live up to all
its actual norms, not just those to which lip service is given. The leader
is a person who "comes closest to realizing the norms the group values
highest. . . . He controls the group, yet he is in a sense more controlled
by it than others are, since it is a condition of his leadership that his actions and decisions shall conform more closely than those of others to an
abstract norm."[10]

This analysis of two natural groups supports the notion, suggested
from Merei's experiment, that adherence to group ideals and traditions is a
condition of leadership. However, the other side of the problem of leadership is the leader's responsibility to initiate and promote change. What
was concluded from the studies of natural groups on this dimension?
Homans, addressing this problem, states that the responsibility of a leader
is "deliberately to bring his group from one social state to another." He
implies, but does not say directly and explicitly, that this is a problem of
change in group norms. His argument implies that the leader's high social
rank and ability to command others create the leverage to change the
group. The behavior of members is changed by the application, or antici-

---

[10]Homans, *The Human Group*, pp. 188–89.

pation, of the leader's sanctions against recalcitrant group members. A leader has recourse to socially punitive actions: A leader can weaken or withdraw personal friendship, lessen the frequency and duration of interactions with a member, decrease the other's social rank, or foster unfavorable attitudes toward the member.

The relevant question is not whether a leader has bases of influence over group members, but rather, when does a leader, in pursuing group change, begin to be seen as no longer representing group traditions? At some point, a leader begins to lose the confidence of members and the ability to influence them. The problem is to maintain one's prestige and yet to change norms from which the prestige is gained.

This dilemma of leadership is based on the fact that groups may have conflicting norms or standards for leaders. While a group may value its traditions and require the leader to adhere to them, it may also expect necessary changes to be proposed and made by the leader. A leader who embodies group ideals but is inattentive to change fails to fulfill group expectations, as does one who meets expectations for making necessary changes in the group but fails to live up to group traditions. Homans states:

> The leader must live up to the norms of the group—all the norms—better than any follower. At the same time, he is the member of the group who is most in danger of violating the norms. In disputes between two followers, he is expected to do justice, as the group understands justice, but what man can always be just? And it is the leader who may sometimes act for the good of the group and still not act wholly acceptably. His action is appropriate to the group norms in one way, but does violence to them in another.[11]

Singular or dominant emphasis on either tradition or change is likely to undermine a leader's confidence and stature with group members. Change and stability are requirements of all enduring groups, and expectations of these conflicting forces are usually present for leaders. These competing directions for leadership action can lead to a constantly shifting relationship between leaders and groups. Especially where a group's environment requires adaptation, the relationship may be more or less at tension or at ease, but it is usually in a state of flux.

Illustrations of Institutional Change in the U.S. Navy

Sideburns, beards, and mustaches.   A recent example of institutional leadership illustrates the problem of instigating change at risk of weaken-

---

[11]Homans, *The Human Group*, p. 427.

ing one's own influence and position. During his tour as U.S. Chief of Naval Operations from 1970 to 1974, Adm. Elmo Zumwalt initiated revision of some of the navy's traditions and codes of conduct. Taking office in 1970, Zumwalt initiated a series of changes in the handling of personnel, including liberalization of dress codes, elimination of demeaning treatment of navy persons, permission for beer dispensers in barracks, improvement of communications between officers and sailors, and an increase in recruitment and improvement of the treatment of minority, especially black, personnel.[12]

In a number of areas, Zumwalt's orders, or "Z-grams," went directly against strong navy tradition, and they provoked heated controversy within the navy. Information about these events, available primarily through news articles, gives a fragmented and incomplete picture of Zumwalt's actions and others' reactions.[13] But it does offer a glimpse of attempted normative change at the level of institutional leadership.

In June 1971, Admiral Zumwalt addressed the graduating class at the U.S. Naval Academy, stating his view of needed adaptation of naval traditions.[14] One of his themes was taken from an address to Annapolis graduates of 1942, in which it was stated that traditions best testify to the ways and accomplishments of earlier naval officers, and that each navy generation must make its own traditions.[15] Zumwalt made a strong plea for updating the navy and relating it to the surrounding society. He said that naval officers cannot be isolated from the rest of the society, that the internal "club" will be secure no more, and that the navy must awaken to its responsibilities in the broader society.[16] It is evident that adaptation of the navy was an important issue for Zumwalt and that his objective was revision of some naval traditions and norms.

Press reports of manpower turnover, if correct, certainly indicated a need for adapting to changing societal values and mores. One report placed the volunteer rate for a second term in all ranks and branches of the services at 31 percent in 1970, the lowest reenlistment rate since 1955.[17] Another report stated that 10 percent of first-term enlisted men in the navy reenlisted, and less than 3 percent reenlisted on aircraft carriers in the Atlantic Fleet.[18] In his speech, Zumwalt was clearly aware

[12]"Humanizing the U.S. Military," *Time*, 96 (December 21, 1970), 16–22.

[13]Richard J. Levine, "A Final Z-Gram From Zumwalt," *Wall Street Journal*, May 13, 1974, p. 14.

[14]Admiral E.R. Zumwalt, Jr., "Personal Accountability: The Demand of New Approaches," *Vital Speeches of the Day*, 37, No. 17 (July 15, 1971), 605–8.

[15]Zumwalt, "Personal Accountability," p. 606.

[16]Zumwalt, "Personal Accountability," p. 607.

[17]"Humanizing," p. 16.

[18]Levine, "A Final Z-gram," p. 14.

of a visible trend of rejection of the services and of downgrading military careers.

But while Zumwalt was initiating change by virtue of his leadership position and expounding on the rationale for institutional adaptation through forums such as the Annapolis commencement address, the questions of norm change by no means had unanimity in the navy. The press reports mentioned above presented the controversy of these reforms within the service and reported the existence of a movement to replace Zumwalt. A weakening or breakdown of discipline was the issue upon which disagreement with reform was focused. Modernization of rules and procedures was seen to threaten another strong value of the navy—a disciplined and obedient fighting force. Racial fights on navy ships and sitdown demonstrations of black crewmen aboard several naval vessels in 1972 reinforced this concern, and led to a House subcommittee investigation of navy "permissiveness."[19] Zumwalt's changes were as readily seen by some as destructive as they were seen by others as adaptive. As they were apparently opposed by older officers and chief petty officers, they were applauded by younger sailors.

The leader, Zumwalt, appeared to be in the middle of a dispute between competing values. He pointed to the historical fact that the practice of flogging had been resisted, for fear of weakening discipline, for thirty years before it was abolished.[20] Yet people did disagree on the need for liberalization. Zumwalt stressed the demand for flexibility, and this stand led to loss of confidence, in at least some quarters, in his leadership.

Perhaps the decision to initiate change was imperative for Zumwalt, in that the problems of naval manpower and social disfavor forced this decision, and that there was no real choice. Yet there were undoubtedly choices about the need for adaptation faced and made by his predecessors. There were choices of the emphasis and comprehensiveness of Zumwalt's thrust for change, too, let alone the extent of his commitment when controversy stirred. Is this example typical or unique? Its main uniqueness may be the degree of publicity it has received; the forces for fostering normative change and stability are opposing forces constantly faced by organizational leaders.

Social norms and technological change. One writer concerned with the adaptation of social systems, especially to technical change, has said that innovators need to have skills at waging "guerrilla warfare" against established systems in order to have their innovations acknowledged and accepted.[21] In this view, organizations do not carry on by the movement

[19]"Zeroing In on Z," *Newsweek*, 80 (December 4, 1972), 29–30.
[20]Zumwalt, "Personal Accountability," p. 607.
[21]Donald A. Schon, *Beyond the Stable State* (New York: Random House, 1971).

of inertia; rather, they "fight to remain the same." They have "dynamic conservatism." Donald Schon, proponent of this view, states:

> Because of its dynamic conservatism, a social system is unlikely to undertake its own change of state. Because it sees every effort at transformation as an attack, transformation becomes a kind of war. Major shifts in the system come about in response to the system's failure or the threat of failure—as political revolution may succeed a period of economic disaster, or as total corporate reorganization may succeed near ruin.[22]

A colorful example of organizational resistance to a dramatic technical innovation is provided by historian Elting Morison, who traced the development of a revolutionary innovation in navy weapon capacity at the beginning of the twentieth century.[23] The technique, called "continuous-aim firing," involved the introduction of an elevating gear that allowed a sailor to keep continuous sight of his target. Formerly, firing was done with a fixed gun mount, and a sailor needed to use his own sense of timing in order to compensate for the roll of the ship. Continuous sighting of a target encouraged the further development and the adoption of telescopic sighting. Morison reports that the effect of these two innovations was such that within six years after their eventual acceptance by the U.S. Navy, firing accuracy had improved 3,000 percent.

What was the process of introduction of this idea into the institutional system of the navy? In 1900, an American officer stationed in China learned of the technique from Percy Scott of the British navy, who had invented the method of firing. The American officer, William Sims, seems to have accepted reform of the U.S. Navy as a personal mission, and he chose continuous-aim firing as his first issue in that reform. Sims adopted the technique on his own ship and then began to document the effectiveness of the method in messages to appropriate officials in Washington. He wrote report after report containing factual and dramatic data on the superiority of this innovation. Morison states that Sims wrote 13 large official reports, to which he received not a single response.

His second tactic involved the use of harsher, more aggressive language and the distribution of his reports out of channels to other officers. These moves generated a response; in Washington, the chief of the Bureau of Ordnance responded with test data (conducted on land!) showing, he said, that Sims's claims were simply impossible.

As a last recourse, Sims wrote to President Theodore Roosevelt to

[22]Schon, *Beyond the Stable State*, p. 55.
[23]Elting E. Morison, *Men, Machines, and Modern Times* (Cambridge, Mass.: M.I.T. Press, 1966), pp. 17–44.

present his case. Roosevelt took a personal interest in Sims and installed him, for the duration of Roosevelt's administration, as naval inspector of target practice, a post from which Sims was able to implement his technique on a service-wide basis.

Why did Sims face such great difficulty in gaining the acknowledgement and acceptance of a new self-evident contribution to naval performance? Morison's answer lies in the analysis of a military institution as a way of life. Beliefs, norms, values, routines, ways of thinking, and social relationships have enduring stability. In the navy, these factors emerge in relation to, and continue to be tied to, the nature of the ship. Technical changes that transform the nature of the ship and the sailors' relation to it impinge upon the norms and organization of this way of life and may threaten its existence. Morison states:

> The opposition, where it occurs, of the soldier and the sailor to such change springs from the normal human instinct to protect oneself and one's way of life. Military organizations are societies built around and upon the prevailing weapons systems. Intuitively and quite correctly the military man feels that a change in weapon portends a change in the arrangements of his society.[24]

The lesson is not that naval officials in Sim's day were resistant to or did not seek technical innovation and change. They were very likely to be, as most managers are today, strongly interested in technical advances. The problem was more that the technical change that Sims presented was spontaneous and unexpected, it originated from an unknown and not particularly credible source, and it would cause substantial alterations in naval procedures and organization. From a broad perspective, the institutional reaction was irrational, but from a closer perspective it was understandable.

It should not, of course, be concluded from the two Navy examples that the problem of social organization and change is that people higher or lower in organization are consistently resisters of innovation. Pressures for change and adaptation can originate anywhere in an organization, and the support or resistance of other parts of the organization is determined by the factors of specific situations.

Presence of the Dilemma in All Change-oriented Roles

This dilemma of the manager in organizational change is also common to other roles involving social change. Any person seeking change must have a basis of legitimacy in the system to be changed, a legitimacy that may

[24]Morison, *Men, Machines, and Modern Times*, pp. 35–36.

be called into question because of the advocacy of change. For example, the crosscultural technical assistant needs to have acceptance before he or she will be taken into the confidence and given the trust of local people. Stories are plentiful of foreign assistance efforts in which newly dug wells were not used, new fertilizers were not applied, or labor-saving machines sat idle. In many of these cases, the foreign assistant, while technically competent, simply did not seek or earn social credibility. This is one type of the bumbling "ugly American." Social norms and values can often be a stronger barrier to economic development than lack of technical know-how. But how does a foreign assistant who places social acceptance and personal relations ahead of technology ever get to the point of introducing technology without losing his or her basis of cultural support? An assistant who wholly goes the social route may become entrapped by the inhibiting customs and mores that need to be changed in the first place. One point of view holds that social conventions have to be violated for significant change to occur, and the foreign assistant ought not to squander his or her resources by "misplaced sentiment." The unwitting "ugly American" is one thing, and a deliberate strategy is another. Charles Savage, author of this view, stated:

> An even more powerful style of intervention achieves the ends of the Ugly American, but does so knowledgeably. Its practitioner understands the old order and the nature of the resistance it offers. He is prepared to accord it limited respect; he is also prepared to tread on local sensibilities when this is what is required.[25]

Build rapport in order to have credibility and influence, or offer new values and models by not bowing to the conventions of the traditional culture? Cultural-change agents must necessarily do both, and the choice one faces in a specific situation may constitute a dilemma.

Additionally, this same type of conflict has been observed in the role of the organizational consultant working in the area of human relations. One organizational-change agent argues that consideration of feelings and emotions of people in work relationships is fundamental to accurate communication and effective decision making. However, feelings and emotions are typically considered by managers as irrelevant to doing the work of the organization. This situation places the consultant in a dilemma about how to choose his or her own behavior—not to deal with emotions at the start of the consulting relationship is more likely to gain the acceptance of the client, but it means foregoing opportunities to

[25]Charles H. Savage, Jr., "Needed: More Ugly Americans," *The Technology Review*, Vol. 67, 7 (1965), 42.

instigate change. On the other hand, to deal with emotions in the relationship with the client creates the possibility of introducing change, but also carries a higher risk of losing the client. The author of this analysis points out:

> The consultant is in a very difficult position. If he behaves according to his ideas and values, he stands a good chance of being a threat to the client. He could be asked to leave. If he decides to behave even temporarily in accordance with the client's values, he may be accepted but he runs a serious risk of failing to change and develop.[26]

The person concerned with change, whether as an administrator, a cross-cultural-change agent, or an organizational consultant, confronts dual responsibilities—to adhere to and to change group norms. While specific accommodations may be made in individual situations, the tension of these two criteria is generally present for the instigator of social change.

The consultant role described above dealt with the place of openness and trust in communication with a client. The degree of openness of communication is also a norm of interaction between manager and work groups. To the degree that greater work accomplishment can be achieved by greater openness of communication, the leader carries a responsibility to foster effective communication. At the same time, changing this norm subjects the leader to personal risk taking akin to that of the organizational consultant in attempting to develop new norms of interaction. This dimension of the manager's role is the focus of the final section of this chapter.

Leadership and Group Norms of Communication

An experiment in group communication.   One organizational requirement for groups is productivity or task accomplishment. Organizational goals are promoted to the extent that human capabilities in groups are fully utilized and productive. Yet, familiar to most people's experience in organizations are norms or patterns of interaction among people involving withholding or inhibition of ideas and expressions. Interpersonal norms of interaction are often such as to militate against the full use of human resources; participation is often adversely influenced by status differences, and unfamiliarity among people often inhibits participation.

---

[26]Chris Argyris, "Explorations in Consulting-Client Relationships," *Human Organization*, Vol. 20, 3 (1961), 123.

Essentially, these phenomena are stability forces in group relations. Expression of thoughts and feelings in a given group tend to stabilize where responses of others are relatively predictable and patterns or norms of communication and participation become established at these points. To the extent that this factor is present, full utilization of human capabilities is restricted, and the organization has a lesser degree of, and perhaps significantly lesser degree of, effectiveness. The description of one relevant laboratory experiment will serve to elaborate the nature of the issue and to highlight the leader's choices relative to this problem.

The relationship between group task performance and interpersonal stability is dramatically illustrated in a laboratory experiment by Marvin Shaw and J. Michael Blum.[27] These two researchers were interested in the concept of "pluralistic ignorance"—a situation in which group members believe incorrectly that others in the group hold a certain attitude, whereas they themselves do not. When pluralistic ignorance exists, members are reluctant to express their views in order to avoid potentially deviant roles. Yet, in fact, there is absolutely nothing deviant about their feelings—other group members share them as well. The problem is that group members feel similarly and yet think they feel differently. For example, pluralistic ignorance exists if all five members of a staff want to cancel a weekly staff meeting, and each person feels alone in this desire. Each person thinks he or she is in the minority and attends the meeting rather than risk being shown as different. Since all attend in this manner, the meeting suffers from uninvolvement, and each person's original assumptions are affirmed.

Where pluralistic ignorance exists, a group has incomplete information for its work, and consequently, the group's effectiveness is reduced. Shaw and Blum postulated that increased awareness of the feelings of others (overcoming pluralistic ignorance) would improve group performance. They also believed that awareness of others' feelings would be more important in the solution of difficult rather than easy tasks, since difficult tasks would put a premium on complete information, expression of all ideas available, exploration of alternatives, and individual involvement.

The concept of pluralistic ignorance is related to the problem of group adaptation and member stability. An organization is likely to be successful when its groups effectively and creatively solve tasks. On the other hand, if the reasoning about pluralistic ignorance is correct, these group outcomes require members to express their ideas and feelings to each other, and this requirement may disturb the equilibrium of group

---

[27]Marvin E. Shaw and J. Michael Blum, "Group Performance as a Function of Task Difficulty and the Group's Awareness of Member Satisfaction," *Journal of Applied Psychology*, 49 (1965), 151–54.

relations. As mentioned earlier, norms of communication in most groups stabilize at a point of less than full participation. The result of this situation is a discrepancy between the ideal needs of the organization and the actual behaviors of group members.

The problem of pluralistic ignorance also has a close relationship to the issues of deviance and conformity discussed in the last chapter. Conformity to a group norm of low expression of ideas and feelings allows pluralistic ignorance to develop and to be maintained. Independent action in this case consists of direct and explicit communication of one's views, regardless of the group. This action would serve to explode the false belief of the group. While this aspect of group norms is similar to the membership/independence dilemma of Chapter 5 for a group member, the present focus is on the relationship of the leader to group norms of this type. Because of an organizational responsibility for group performance, this situation has additional complications for the leader.

Shaw and Blum designed an experiment to study whether member awareness of group satisfaction would increase group effectiveness, and whether this effect was more pronounced for difficult than for easy group tasks. They invented a satisfaction-feedback device, a "moraleometer," to vary members' awareness of group satisfaction. The moraleometer was a box with 25 light bulbs in it that sat in the middle of the table around which a five-person group was arranged. Five bulbs were each connected to a switch control located at each group member's position. By moving the switch from 1 to 5, each member could control the number of lights lit up in the middle of the table, thus expressing to the other group members a particular level of satisfaction at that moment. The total number of lights lit up at any one time reflected the degree of group satisfaction.

In addition, the moraleometer was arranged so that each person's expression of satisfaction could or could not be individually identified by the other group members. For some groups, the level of each person's satisfaction would be specifically known, and for other groups, only the group aggregate would be known. There were three conditions of feedback: *no feedback*, in which the moraleometer was not used; *covert feedback*, in which only aggregate satisfaction was identifiable; and *overt feedback*, in which individual expressions were also identifiable. These three feedback conditions were established across three different group tasks that varied from easy to difficult.

The results of the experiment turned out as predicted. On all three tasks, group performance was higher when satisfaction feedback was present than when it was not. Thus, member awareness of group satisfaction had a definite impact on increasing group performance, and the experiment suggested that overcoming pluralistic ignorance promotes group problem solving. To the extent that members were aware of others' satisfaction, they were more able to know the relationship of their own and others' feelings. Knowing the level of group satisfaction apparently helped people participate more fully, and this led to better task solutions.

Some interesting results were found by comparison of the feedback conditions. First, group performance on the most difficult task for the covert-feedback group was significantly higher than for the overt-feedback group. The other two tasks showed no significant differences in task performance between these feedback conditions. Second, each person, at the end of the experiment, anonymously filled out a questionnaire that measured overall satisfaction with the group's work. This overall-satisfaction index was then correlated with the average number of lights each person had indicated to the group during the experiment. It turned out that the average number of lights shown by those in the covert condition correlated better with the overall-satisfaction index than did the average number of lights shown by those in the overt condition. In other words, people gave a more valid reflection of their actual satisfaction in the covert-feedback condition. Even in this experiment, personal identification with the number of lights lit seemed to inhibit true expression of feelings of satisfaction. Supporting this view was the fact that the range of indicated satisfaction on the moraleometer for overt feedback was significantly less than for covert feedback.

If knowledge of members' feelings is instrumental to group performance on difficult tasks, and if covert feedback obtained more accurate readings of satisfaction than overt feedback, one is not surprised that the experimenters found group performance higher in covert than overt conditions. But what relation does this result have to behavior in organizations? In real life, there is no covert-feedback condition as designed in this experiment. There are, of course, nonverbal and thus covert indications of satisfaction, but these are more ambiguous and incomplete in most settings than in the covert-feedback condition of this experiment. Also, the overt-feedback condition was not as "risky" as overt feedback in work-related interaction. It should be considerably easier to reflect a level of satisfaction different from that of others through a set of lights than to express one's difference verbally. Communicating satisfaction covertly in everyday organizational experience is less likely to be as clear and effective as in the experiment, and communicating overt satisfaction feedback is riskier. This makes it more important and less probable that the necessary communication will occur naturally.

Implications for a group leader. The groups in Shaw and Blum's experiments had no designated leaders. What, if any, inferences might be made from this experiment to organizations in which groups typically have formal leaders? First, it is reasonable to assume that other areas of participation in groups, such as suggesting new or different ideas, are subject to the same inhibiting effect of groups as was the expression of satisfaction in the experiment. Second, one might also reason that a group leader, being a person, experiences the same personal force toward stability of equilibrium of group relations. In other words, a leader, regardless of, and perhaps because of, the status of the position, may be inclined not to participate fully in "overt" group discussion. Why would not the same forces that allowed group members in the experiment to be more "honest" in covert feedback apply as well to leaders in real organizational groups?

If this inference is correct, a leader, who carries official organizational responsibility for group performance, may be inclined to act in ways that decrease this performance. Participating fully would seem, at a minimum, to carry the same risk for a leader as for a group member. In fact, the risk of appearing different or out of bounds with an idea may be even more greatly experienced by a leader. On the one hand, a group leader stands to secure personal needs in group relations at the possible risk of detriment to official role obligations, and on the other hand, he or she stands to fulfill the requirements of the organizational role at the expense of personal needs. To the extent that there is a need for high performance on a difficult group task, and to the extent that the group leader follows typical patterns of group relations, this situation becomes a dilemma.

CHAPTER REVIEW

This chapter has reviewed leaders in a variety of organizational and group settings. We have discussed leaders in farming neighborhoods in Kentucky, children placed as "leaders" into nursery-school groups, Taylor as an emerging work group leader, and Doc as the leader of a street gang. We have also touched upon organizational leadership through two examples from the U.S. Navy, the first involving change of social customs and traditions, and the second involving introduction of a technical innovation.

The first observation from these examples concerns the leader's relationship to group norms and traditions. In each case, leaders had a strong obligation to live up to, if not the ideals, at least the expectations of group norms. Group members seem to want to experience a leader not only as one of them, but as one of the best of them.

A second point is that the norms, customs, and traditions of a group or organization are factors of stability. They are usually closely tied to the past and serve the useful purposes of continuity and predictability. A leadership dilemma arises when social, economic, or technical factors external to the group create a necessity for the group's norms to change and adapt to the new circumstances of the group. These times, which are perceived to be increasingly salient in contemporary society, can give rise to a dilemma of leadership: How does a person do what is essential in a position of leadership—namely, adhere to the group's norms and traditions—and fulfill the obligation of the leadership position to change those norms in needed ways? It appears that a leader has only so much "idiosyncrasy credit" to expend in change activities before risking the confidence of group members.

Another aspect of this dilemma has been noted. The study of a technical innovation showed how closely related social mores and organization can be to the nature of physical, technical objects such as ships and weapons systems. Adopting technical improvements and advances is usually not a decision based on technical merit alone, but one that has ramifications for established and stable, and therefore desirable, ways of life. A dilemma may arise when such pleasant stability conflicts with necessities for organizational development in a changing society and world. The tension between technical innovation and social mores was seen to be present also in the role of cross-cultural technical assistant, and the general issue of stability versus change was seen as present in the role of organizational consultant.

Finally, group norms of communication at suboptimal levels for work performance were seen to result from group members' needs for relatively familiar, predictable, and stable interaction. This finding was thought to apply to the leader's situation, in that leaders have the same personal needs for familiarity in group relations. And yet leaders, also carrying official organizational responsibility for group performance, may experience a dilemma of action. This dilemma is expected to be present as tasks are difficult and require group effort, and as the people involved follow typical patterns of interaction.

The leadership dilemma discussed in this chapter is obviously more salient as external pressures for change and internal pressures for performance increase. In a stable, relatively uncompetitive environment, the tension of adhering to and changing group norms is unlikely to be significant. In addition, a number of other factors—such as the immediacy for change, the imbeddedness of group traditions, and the prestige and security of the leader—will all influence the extent to which this potential dilemma is experienced.

Yet all organizations and groups are normative systems that have traditions, values, and stable, time-honored procedures, and today's society is anything but placid in the degree of social, economic, technological, and political change. The dilemma of adhering to and changing organizational norms, if not widely present now, is likely to become a familiar experience of organizational leadership. Managers will more and more be required to meet the twin requirements for organizational change and organizational stability, to be both symbol of time-honored traditions and change agent for the future. In managing groups, administrators will increasingly be called upon to balance, integrate, or combine their organizational responsibilities with personal needs for stable work relationships. The impact of these forces is likely to be left by managers as a direct function of the general rate of national and global change.

Chapter 7

Directions
for Managing Dilemmas

Administration calls for a manager to be an individualist and a collectivist, a commander and a counsellor, a dispassionate official and a passionate human associate, a group member and an individual conscience, a supporter of tradition and an agent of social change. Administrative behavior involves a diversity of roles emphasizing different criteria for action, and administrative situations inevitably arise in which some of these criteria are in conflict with others.

The preceding five chapters have positioned the manager on the horns of these dilemmas. The present chapter discusses several ways to guide people through this process of choice. First, we will recap the dilemma situations that have been discussed, then we will turn to the question of what guides may be available to help the manager cope with dilemmas. Finally, the existential nature of choice in administrative behavior will be explored.

Recapitulation

The five dilemmas of administrative behavior presented in this book were described as conflicts relating the individual either to the organization as a whole or to the face-to-face group. Within the first area, it was argued that certain organizational expectations or obligations are part of any administrative role: to act in the interests of the whole, to apply authority in relation to subordinates so that prescribed work is accomplished and organizational direction is maintained and to enhance "organizationally" important values of economy and equity. The preservation and growth of an organization depends on the realization of these obligations by its members. Failure to act as if organizations are concrete realities would undermine their existence.

Tension is given to administrative choice by the consistent presence of criteria conflicting with these. Where the individual faces collective responsibility, there is also responsibility to his or her personal goals; where authoritative control is needed, individual growth and rights are also desired; where economy and equity are called for, dignity and individualization are needed.

These dilemmas are not conflicts between "what I want to do" and "what others expect of me." Rather, role obligations are internal to each of us in the process of administration. The conflict of these dilemmas is more aptly described as "what I can do for fulfillment of my personal attitudes, beliefs and needs," versus "what I can do for fulfillment of myself in an organizational position."

In addition to a conflict between a role criterion and a personal criterion in these three chapters, each chapter was also concerned with the problem of ends and means. Individual purposes cannot be fulfilled in the absence of organizations. In this sense, the collectivity is a means to the realization of individuals. However, maintenance of the collectivity cannot be satisfied without ordering and constraining the actions of individuals. In this sense, the individual is a means to the survival of the collectivity, which, we have just said, is a means to individual fulfillment. This ironic relation of individuals and organizations gives rise to conflicts of criteria in here-and-now decisions: Both organizational and individual criteria are valid, and each can justifiably be claimed as an immediate value. Whether the issue is multiple responsibilities, authority, or organizational versus personal criteria, the knotty problem of ends and means is present in administrative behavior.

The second major focus of the book has been on the individual as a member of face-to-face groups. The basic fact here is that groups are normative systems—their various prescriptions for members' behavior are a source of continuity and cohesion that is necessary for social relations. At the same time, the normative prescriptions in groups present individuals with the problems of establishing areas of personal independence in relation to group norms and of fostering normative change necessary for group adaptation. In the first of these problems, a person may face conflicting personal needs: on the one hand, a desire for the emotional satisfactions of membership and inclusion, and on the other hand, a desire to maintain a high degree of independent judgment and action. The latter problem is a conflict centering on dual meanings of leadership: In one instance, leadership can be representing the ideals and values of a group, and in another instance, it can be changing these ideals and values in the light of external circumstances. In both these problems, dilemmas arise for the individual in relation to a group when either the two personal needs or the two leadership requirements are experienced simultaneously.

The terms of these dilemmas—for example, collective responsibility, organizational hierarchy, or group norms—have largely been treated as independent and distinct concepts. But, as is the case in much of behavioral science, terms are not entirely discrete, and meanings are relative to specific usage. The possible interrelations of the concepts in this book are complex. Organizational hierarchy has been discussed as a means of ensuring a minimal level of collective action. Similarly, supporting group norms may in a specific situation be tantamount to assuming collective responsibility. The specific meaning of these and other terms depends to some extent on the situation in which they are used.

For this reason, the administrative dilemmas discussed here are not presented as the definition of a field or as conclusive statements on the substance of administration. The present way of organizing dilemmas is suggestive rather than definitive. It offers a way of thinking about dilemmas in administrative behavior, rather than providing a confirmed set of categories into which all experience need fit.

This book, based on the belief that "an organization is different from the sum of its members," has proposed that genuine dilemmas are a salient dimension in the practice of management. However, the exact nature of a dilemma for any one manager at any particular time may best be described in unique terms and specific circumstances. The conclusions of this analysis relate to the inherent, but general, tension of organizational and individual criteria in management: Conclusions about the actual experience of managing need to be drawn by practicing managers and students of administration. This book has sought a fresh approach by which people can examine their experiences and choices in administration. It is hoped that the discussions of the five dilemmas provide some convenient and thought-provoking entry points into this area.

Guidelines for Managing Dilemmas

Administrative behavior is typically phrased by academicians and practitioners in terms of single roles or a single criterion for decision. For example, management is often viewed from only an individualistic framework, or from the standpoint of control, or solely within the criteria of costs and economy. This way of thinking is based on the assumption that single best answers to managerial problems are available and will ultimately be discovered. Yet, to the extent that administrative situations are multifaceted, effective decision making needs to account for more than single criteria. The real questions may be how to promote individual *and* collective interests, how to exercise control *and* gain initiative, or how to have an efficient cost structure *and* promote individuality, and so forth.

Achieving multiple criteria means the manager must be able to play numerous roles and use many criteria for decisions. It means that no course can be blocked by habit or lack of attention.

When administrative dilemmas are experienced in administrative behavior, what guides and ideas foster the use of multiple criteria? How does this concept lead a person to cope with an administrative dilemma? Although the inherent nature of a dilemma prevents a "solution" in the conventional sense, perhaps some guidance, help, or advice can be given to managers in addressing these situations. We will first consider several ways in which a person might be oriented to the process of choice. The most useful orientation is a position of "interested neutrality" within a field of potential actions. In this stance, one is unconstrained by *a priori* mental sets, habits, or a need for consistency, and can freely direct personal energy into the immediate situation.

Second, in grappling with a dilemma, a person may come to see a way of preventing future dilemmas from arising in the same situation. It may be possible in some situations to act to change the conditions giving rise to a dilemma. The concept of the "invention of concrete solutions" may be a guide to the administrative practitioner in considering an approach to dilemmas.

Orienting oneself to choice.   Dilemmas have been presented in this book as situations of competing criteria, acting as opposing forces on an individual. Yet the way in which these forces are considered to oppose one another is a significant factor in whether the resulting tension is productive and possibly creative, or whether it is debilitating. The way a person reacts to administrative dilemmas might focus and release energy or constrain it.

Conceptual work about fields of forces comes from the study of individual and group decision making in gestalt psychology. In the application of gestalt principles to human development, the personality is thought to comprise many parts, each of which is often in conflict with another.[1] For every want or need there is often an opposing force, or "resister," that creates conflict and ambivalence within the person. Action

---

[1]Frederick Perls, Ralph F. Hefferline, and Paul Goodman, *Gestalt Therapy: Excitement and Growth in the Human Personality* (New York: Dell, 1951), p. 44.

is an expression of the equilibrium established between forces. The tension of these forces is often manifest in feelings of tiredness, or loss of interest and excitement. The task of personal development in this case—and, by extrapolation, the task of coping with administrative dilemmas—is to free one's energy from the tension-creating conflict, making it available for constructive and creative expression.

An example of this equilibrium of forces comes from Kurt Lewin's studies of patterns of food consumption and buying habits during the Second World War.[2] Lewin's ultimate objective was to develop knowledge of how food habits might be influenced to increase the use of beef hearts, sweetbreads, and kidneys toward greater food utilization. In these studies, Lewin characterized the buying of food as a conflict situation composed of opposing forces. For example, a given food might be very desirable to the buyer, exerting a force to buy, but also very expensive, exerting a counterforce to not buy. In this case, the part of the consumer's personality that wants to buy is resisted by a part that doesn't want to buy. Other forces to buy or not buy a particular food might exist, such as nutritional criteria, tastes of others in the family, difficulty or ease of preparation, the appropriateness of the food to the occasion, and so forth. A model of such a situation of opposing forces is:

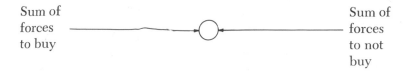

Sum of forces to buy ——————— ○ ← ——————— Sum of forces to not buy

Lewin states the following rule of decision: "Food is bought if the total force toward buying becomes greater than the opposing forces until the food basket is filled." In other words, a decision is an outcome of the relative strength of opposing forces.

Lewin extended this concept of forces into group behavior as well. Here he observed that any particular aspect of behavior, such as a level of productivity, is a function of a complex interaction of opposing forces. A given level of productivity in a group is the point at which forces for raising and for lowering productivity are balanced. Furthermore, as the level of productivity goes up, the forces against raising it become stronger, and as the level goes down, the forces against lowering it become stronger. Lewin called this principle of system behavior a *quasi stationary equilibrium.*

The two aspects of a dilemma are neatly balanced forces on

[2]Kurt Lewin, "Group Decision and Social Change," in *Readings in Social Psycho* eds. Eleanor E. Maccoby, Theodore M. Newcomb, and Eugene L. Hartley (New Holt, Rinehart, & Winston, 1958), pp. 197–211.

person in a given situation. In a true dilemma, the "buy" and "not buy" forces are perfectly equal. The principle of a quasi-stationary equilibrium applies to this situation; as one moves toward one side of the decision, the forces toward the other side become stronger, pushing the decision back to the center point.

The nature of an internal conflict or of an administrative dilemma is the presence of a position that has merit, opposed by another position also with merit. Because of training, habit, or possibly the need to avoid ambiguity, people fall into a "taking of sides," where one side of the situation is favored at the expense of the other. In the example of patterns of food consumption, people establish habitual buying patterns in which some criteria are consistently dominant over others. Each opponent in an interpersonal conflict usually has a valid complaint against the other, each political party has a potentially useful social contribution to make, each of several conflicting wants within a person is important. Each side contains a truth or a part truth; but each side is, in itself, also an incomplete truth. The greatest barrier to resolving conflicts is inflexibility as consistency of behavior is a strongly ingrained cultural precept. One contemporary psychologist points out:

> In most cultures, consistency, if it is not prized in and for itself, is certainly reinforced as a general behavior underlying a multitude of specific responses. In our society, the "golden rule" stresses interpersonal consistency, the hypocrite is derided because his actions are inconsistent with his words, our child-rearing practices build consistency into almost every aspect of human functioning, and our educational systems emphasize logical consistency and historical continuity.[3]

The gestalt approach in human development is to break habitual and consistent ways of experiencing and perceiving: One seeks to imagine and accept the opposite of accustomed ways of thinking and choosing. Unfamiliar and unconventional experiencing is sought to orient the individual differently to the immediate context. With a capacity to experience opposites, the person is less the center of centripetal forces and becomes the center of centrifugal forces, such as:

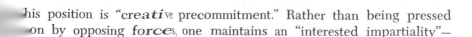

his position is "creative precommitment." Rather than being pressed on by opposing forces, one maintains an "interested impartiality"—

p G. Zimbardo, *The Cognitive Control of Motivation: The Consequences of ? and Dissonance* (Glenville, Ill.: Scott, Foresman, 1969), p. 280.

ready for action, fully experiencing the opposites, but uncommitted as yet to a position. This stance frees energy from the debilitating aspect of taking sides and encourages a unique response to the special circumstances:

> *"Creative pre-commitment"* is the situation of being ... poised between but *aware of and interested in the potential situations which extend in either direction.* One feels the beckonings to action, but is not yet committed to either side.[4]

Creative precommitment is a guide to decision making in dilemma situations. It means not making every decision in advance of the specific situation. A manager is just as likely to act on self-interest as on collective responsibility, on the principle of control or the value of development, as group member or as independent agent, and so forth, in any given circumstance. This concept implies that the manager has a varied repertoire of roles and decision criteria, none of which has a general *a priori* commitment and any of which might be realized in a specific situation. This freedom of response focuses one's energy on the immediate situation rather than tying it up in an internal war of forces. This involved-but-neutral stance permits, even encourages, the realization of multiple criteria in administration. Although this concept does not prescribe the outcome of choice, it may guide the process of choice. A manager who is able to be involved in the situation although not committed *a priori* to either choice stands to experience dilemmas of administrative behavior as challenging and enlivening, and not tiring and difficult.

The role of ambiguity. There is another key to achieving a stance of creative precommitment. Even though the "taking of sides" in a mental and emotional sense in dilemma situations has the disadvantage of heightening tension and blocking movement, it has the apparent advantage of providing certainty of one's position. The experience of creative precommitment, on the other hand, is inherently ambiguous—uncertainty is great as one is involved but temporarily uncommitted. The presence of ambiguity in action is the basis for interest and excitement in choice. The certainty of an *a priori* commitment lacks this potential.

The role of ambiguity in the process of management has been nearly neglected in research on administration. One study, which stands as a strong exception to this trend, showed that ambiguity was a major element of management decision and concluded that it is a selective force determining those who will succeed and those who will fail. Coping with uncertainty and ambiguity requires an advanced stage of personal action

---

[4]Perls, Hefferline, and Goodman, *Gestalt Therapy*, p. 44.

where the manager is untied to preconceived and absolute notions of right and wrong. Melville Dalton, author of this study, stated his view of the successful manager's ability to deal in the vast complexity of organizational processes:

> ... He has become able to consider and deal with all the conflicting interests and values around him. He has in effect become a plurality under one skin. Inconsistency is less of a hobgoblin to him.[5]

One guide to managers in confronting dilemmas is the ability to ask questions that orient themselves to the process of choice. For example: Am I open to holding any one of a variety of roles in this situation and to acting on any one of a variety of criteria, or am I partial, *a priori*, to a particular role and decision criterion? Have I trapped myself in a battle of forces, or am I free to choose in either direction based only on my relationship to the immediate situation? To what extent are my habits, my need for consistency, and my desire to avoid ambiguity influencing my process of choice in this situation? A self-orienting capacity is a primary means of coping with dilemmas and a way of allowing the experience of choice to be fulfilling rather than diminishing.

The invention of creative solutions.   A guide to the solution of practical dilemmas was given by Chester Barnard, a seminal thinker in adminstrative theory. Barnard saw the need to grapple with conflicts of interests and responsibilities as the highest level of executive responsibility. In fact, he argued that the leader's approach to these issues sets the tone and character of an entire organization. Of special interest here is Barnard's insight into how the experience of a dilemma may create the drive to discover or invent another approach that does not have the same difficult qualities. He points to the dilemma created by using certain medicinal drugs, such as cocaine, a number of years ago. Although cocaine had value as a narcotic in the treatment of patients, its side effects were extremely dangerous or even fatal to patients, confronting physicians with a dilemma in its use. However, this problem may have been a strong force in the development of an alternative drug, novocaine, having similar positive effects without the harmful byproduct. This ability to discover a way out of a dilemma is what Barnard terms the "invention of concrete solutions."[6]

While some concrete solutions may be invented at the moment one faces a dilemma, it is likely that we are most often led to act differently

---

[5]Melville Dalton, *Men Who Manage: Fusions of Feeling and Theory in Administration* (New York: John Wiley, 1959), p. 254.

[6]Chester I. Barnard, "Elementary Conditions of Business Morals," *California Management Review*, Fall 1958, pp. 1–13.

in the future in order to avert facing the same dilemma again, as illustrated by the example of novocaine. An example of a company manager from a business teaching case serves to illustrate this point in an administrative context:

> Bob Kendall was departmental manager in an industrial company. One of the products in his department was a product consisting of the equipment and chemical material used to extinguish fires. A recent technical development, this product looked to many executives as a promising area of growth and profitability. However, over the five years of the product's life, it had returned only losses to the company.
>
> The product had a number of problems, including both a market and a production process new to the company. In order to learn more about the production difficulties, Kendall asked for a study of the existing plant of a young and enthusiastic facilities planner in his department.
>
> This facilities planner became highly committed to the idea of a new and modern plant to produce this product. Although his conclusions were based on very partial and questionable assumptions, his enthusiasm and persistence overcame Kendall's reservations and he allowed the planner to propose the multi-million-dollar project to the finance committee of the company. At this level, the executives' general enthusiasm for the product led them away from a close scrutiny of the proposal and it was accepted.
>
> Bob Kendall is now faced with a dilemma: In his own judgment, effort on the product should go into market development and into making the product profitable. In his judgment, the building project ought to be cancelled. This action would, in his view, be in the best interest of the company. On the other hand, he stands to generate strong negative feelings in others by this action. Clearly, the planner thinks this is an absurd idea, and the executives who approved the project are likely to recoil at this decision. Kendall's personal security and career interests indicate he should go along with the decision as made.[7]

In the immediate situation, Bob Kendall confronts a choice in which each alternative has a deleterious side effect. Canceling the project endangers his position and career; not canceling it violates his obligation as a responsible company manager. Perhaps Kendall might invent an immediate solution to this dilemma—such as postponing the project for a year, or scaling down the new plant—but a completely satisfactory

---

[7]"Industrial Products, Inc.," in *Business Policy: Text and Cases*, 3rd ed., eds. C. Roland Christensen, Kenneth R. Andrews, and Joseph L. Bower (Homewood, Ill.: Richard D. Irwin, 1973), pp. 850–61.

solution is unlikely. The real question is, What can he do to avoid getting in these situations in the future? This is where real learning and a true solution are needed.

Perhaps an invention for Kendall would be to prevent any similar proposal from going to the finance committee until he was personally convinced of its merit. Kendall appears caught in this dilemma primarily owing to his inaction, rather than as a result of an inevitable course of events. A specific choice of this type might be averted by his own formulation of a concrete plan for the product that includes marketing and production aspects. Giving his own direction to the product may be a way to align personal interests and his view of the company's interests. This "solution" does not deny the need for his choice in the immediate situation as it had developed. Nor does it imply that his future course will be free of other situations involving conflicting criteria of decision. Kendall's situation is presented to illustrate that a dilemma might provide an insight about how to focus and direct one's efforts in future events.

Again, several questions may help a manager approach the invention of concrete solutions to a dilemma. For example, one might ask, "What type of proposal, product, or action on my part would help avert this situation from arising again?" "What is the role of my own actions in this situation as it has evolved into an administrative dilemma?" "What are the characteristics of an 'ideal' solution, and what actions are necessary to develop it for the future?" This type of orientation places dilemma situations in a context of time and a flow of events and challenges the manager to be an innovator and inventor in administrative practice.

The Significance of Existential Choice in Administration

A final guide to managers is a perspective that touches the philosophical dimension of administration. Choice is, of course, an important question in various life philosophies—it would be remiss to treat dilemmas solely as practical matters. It may be useful to place administration in a broader context of what one might see as a larger human scheme or purpose.

"Out of the void comes the spirit that shapes the ends of men," wrote Chester Barnard of the executive function.[8] The "void," he was saying, is the potential for executive action within the multiple facets of organizations. There are no given ends or purposes in organizations— organizations are instruments of human design. Jean-Paul Sartre stated the view that reality is not created, nor do values exist, except in action.

[8]Chester I. Barnard, *The Functions of the Executive* (Cambridge, Mass.: Harvard University Press, 1938), p. 284.

In the choice of purpose, meaning is created, and actions taken in the area of conflicting interests and criteria determine values. Coping with dilemmas *is* acting, choosing, and creating. The question about dilemmas is not so much how to decide, but rather what values and realities are created by a decision.

Is it possible that a dilemma may be a barrier to action; might not the anguish and despair of decision imply a withdrawal from the struggle of choosing and lead to inactivity? Might not existentialism lead to apathy rather than action? Similarly, one critic of the gestalt "creative precommitment" said, "The attitude of seeing both sides ultimately results in an aloofness from reality."[9] Aloofness, apathy, and inaction are not the consequences of choice, but of a misinterpretation of the fact of choice. Sartre states that inactivity is the antithesis of existence, and Perls states that "pitting one argument against another" can be an excuse for taking action. It is a person's need to be aloof that leads to viewing choice in this way, rather than the opposition of forces leading to aloofness.

In the sphere of administration, one might be tempted to mask inaction with the terminology of a dilemma. However, dilemmas of administrative behavior call for involvement and not aloofness from decision. Apathy arises from an impulse to withdraw and not from the requirements of a dilemma. One may be tempted to treat situations calling for difficult and unpopular decisions as dilemmas. When the motive is to avoid action, however, these are likely to be false dilemmas, which the manager needs an ability to avoid.

If administrative behavior were predetermined, certain, and completely predictable, management might be a rather dusty and uninteresting affair; uncertainty and ambiguity create a richness and challenge to administration. While too much uncertainty may be a threat to sanity, too little is a threat to individual commitment and purpose. Only in the face of choice does purposefulness arise.

Some philosophers perceive an "existential vacuum" in modern society, in which the worthiness or purpose of life is questioned. The quest for meaning may be one of the dominant marks of industrially advanced societies as achieving personal significance may be increasingly difficult in populous, highly automated, and large-scale societies. Viktor Frankl, a former prisoner in a Nazi concentration camp, sees a will to meaning as the primary motivational force for human life.[10] For Frankl, the discovery of meaning and purpose is not related to any particular condition or ex-

[9]Perls, Hefferline, and Goodman, *Gestalt Therapy*, p. 50.
[10]Viktor E. Frankl, *Man's Search for Meaning*, rev. ed. (New York: Simon & Schuster, Touchstone, 1962.)

perience or belief. Frankl quotes Nietzsche's statement, "He who has a *why* to live for can bear with almost any *how*," to suggest that a person's attitude is more important than his or her material condition.

Meaning or purpose is not given—it must be discovered or created separately and independently by each person. Existentialists confront the absence of an externally imposed meaning to life and see in this void the presence of choice and autonomy. The unique human opportunity is to act within this ambiguity to create a personally significant purpose. James Bugenthal, an existential psychologist, conveys the issue in this way:

> Were an ultimate meaning proven, we would be the creatures of that meaning. We would lose one of the most distinctive features of our lives, our autonomy.
>
> The experience of emptiness and meaninglessness to the universe, which is of the same stuff with our personal experience of uncertainty, is also integral to our having choice. Where there is no uncertainty there is no choice. The confrontation of alternatives, of ambiguity, is inherent in having individual autonomy.[11]

This viewpoint is demonstrated in Frankl's life and experiences in Nazi concentration camps in Germany, experiences through which his own views on the search for and possibilities of meaning in life were developed. A person entering camp was first confronted with giving up all material and social symbols, and all affective ties. People were then placed in a life where arbitrary brutality and violence were paramount, and death was commonplace. Conditions of living were despicable, food was inadequate, and medical care virtually nonexistent, and physical demands of work were excessive. The predominant experiences of inmates were fear, exhaustion, illness, semistarvation, and pain. This situation, which stripped away all their former symbols of value and purpose, confronted them with ultimate questions of their existence. In Frankl's account, the central question became, What is there to live for? or, What is the meaning of life?

The issue of life or death in these conditions depended, in part, on the presence of the spirit or intention to live. All external values had disappeared; those who lived discovered an inner value to give them hope. To many, the futility and despair of the situation offered no opportunity for choice, no basis of meaning. Yet, in Frankl's view, there were different ways people could respond, there were paths to meaning and purpose. There was, in short, choice. He states:

[11]James F.T. Bugenthal, *The Science of the Sky* (Cambridge, Mass.: Harvard Business School, adapted from a presentation of Sept. 4, 1965, p. 10).

... Everything can be taken from a man but one thing: the last of the human freedoms—to choose one's attitude in any given set of circumstances, to choose one's own way.[12]

He argues that action was not predetermined or programmed—that while the camp exerted a tremendous influence on people, in the end one's behavior was the result of an inner decision:

Every day, every hour, offered the opportunity to make a decision, a decision which determined whether you would or would not submit to those powers which threatened to rob you of your self, your inner freedom; which determined whether or not you would become the plaything of circumstance, renouncing freedom and dignity to become molded into the form of the typical inmate.[13]

To people today, looking back on the reports of Frankl and others, facing the mental and physical duress of a concentration camp may appear a tremendous challenge in which the opportunity for meaning was great. Yet Frankl states that most prisoners believed the opportunities and challenges of life were in the past rather than the present. A majority of them looked upon the camp as lacking consequence and as meaningless. It is implied that many prisoners longed for the experiences and external values that are present in the day-to-day context of organizational life.

This comparison suggests that the perception of choice is relative to one's circumstances. It may be easier to understand the challenge and opportunity for meaning from a detached position than it is to realize and act on one's choices when intimately involved. And yet, Frankl's statement of the final human freedom—"to choose one's attitude in any given set of circumstances"—appears to apply to all life situations.

The dilemma situations described in this book are only a few of the many circumstances in which managers are called upon to take an attitude, to make a choice. They are, however, situations for which it is more difficult to have recourse to an external frame of reference that specifies what one's attitude in the circumstances *should* be. In this sense, dilemmas of administrative behavior may be decisions that afford a clearer affirmation of human freedom. The ultimate challenge of managing modern organizations may be to maintain this broader perception of the significance of choice while continuing to be involved in the concrete events of administration. The closeness to events creates the necessity for action; the broader perspective gives action a human significance.

[12]Frankl, *Man's Search for Meaning*, p. 65.
[13]Frankl, *Man's Search for Meaning*, pp. 65–66.